I0178343

THE O. J. SIMPSON MURDER CASE

THE STORY OF A MYSTERY WOMAN

THE O. J. SIMPSON MURDER CASE

THE STORY OF A MYSTERY WOMAN

TARA PERSAUD

The O. J. Simpson Murder Case
The Story of a Mystery Woman

Take note that the name Satan and related names are not capitalized. We choose not to acknowledge him, even to the point of violating grammatical rules.

Treasure House An Imprint of Destiny Image® Publishers, Inc. P.O. Box 3 10 Shippensburg, PA 17257-0310

"For where your treasure is, there will your heart be also." Matthew 6:21

ISBN: 9781560432807

For Worldwide Distribution Printed in the USA.

This book and all other Destiny Image and Treasure House books are available at Christian bookstores and distributors worldwide.

For a US. bookstore nearest you, call 1-800-722-67 74. For more information on foreign distributors, call 717-532-3040. Or reach us on the Internet: http://www.reapemet.com

DEDICATION

I dedicate this book to my daughters: To my beloved Shelley, who now awaits me at the Master's side, and to my youngest daughter, Roxanne, who has stood with me through all the days and months since Shelley's untimely death.

I also dedicate this book to the memory of Nicole Brown Simpson and Ronald Goldman, as well as to the grieving members of the Brown family, the Goldman family, and the Simpson family. May God's measureless grace and love enfold and keep them.

Finally, I dedicate this book and my continuing prayers to the victims of violent crimes and to their families. I tasted the bitter pain of loss when my oldest daughter was violently murdered, and my heart goes out to everyone who has been traumatized by violence and loss. Only God truly knows the depth of your pain, and if you can bear to hear it, only He can bring healing to your broken heart and emotions.

CONTENTS

THE O. J. SIMPSON MURDER CASE

THE STORY OF A MYSTERY WOMAN

PREFACE

Throughout this book, I speak of "God having His way" in the OJ. Simpson double-murder case. This requires some frank explanation. As I understand it today, this phrase does not refer so much to the verdict *for* 0. J. Simpson as to the verdict *against the nation*. The most revered institutions of the United States, institutions that traditionally mirror the moral and ethical standards of her people, were "found wanting in the balances" and declared guilty by all witnesses to the spectacle in Los Angeles. Unrest and discontent are not always bad or evil; in this case, these conditions serve as a clear warning to a nation on the verge of self-destruction and disintegration through self-indulgence.

As for 0. J. Simpson's guilt or innocence, I must clearly state that God sent me as a neutral emissary with a mandate to pray for all parties involved in the case. This included Judge Lance Ito and his staff, all the attorneys for the prosecution and the defense, the defendant and his immediate family, and the grieving family members and friends of the two murder victims.

At no time did I have the freedom to "take sides" in the case proceedings or favor one verdict over another, despite the fact that the personal tragedy of my own daughter's violent death would appear to create a bias against any male defendant accused of murdering a woman.

CHAPTER 1

The Prayer

O. J. Simpson had already taken his seat, flanked by attorneys Johnnie Cochran, Jr., and Robert Shapiro, and the rest of the defense attorneys on his "Dream Team." The prosecution team was also seated and shuffling through documents in preparation for a new round of grueling proceedings, and Judge Ito had his well-worn gavel in hand. He was about to reconvene one of the most famous court cases in American history when a woman quietly slipped from her back-row seat in the gallery and bowed to her knees in the center aisle only a few feet from the gate leading to the attorneys' tables.

As a stunned judge Ito looked on, the well-dressed woman began to pray in a resonating voice before the live television camera and microphones. "Father, Father; I am asking You in Jesus' name to open the heavens and give peace and strength to this court." Judge Ito made no move to silence the woman identified as Tara Persaud, a visitor to the Criminal Courts Building. 0. J. Simpson turned around in his seat to see who was praying, and smiled when he heard the concluding words of her prayer. Johnnie Cochran, Jr., and Robert Shapiro both located the woman and smiled, as did Marcia Clark, Christopher Darden, and the rest of the prosecution team.

Although several newspaper reports and "O. J. books" erroneously stated that Persaud "had no ticket" to the high security area and was abruptly hauled away by sheriff's deputies, the Los Angeles newspapers correctly reported that the woman was allowed to say her prayer without interruption before she quietly stood up and walked out of the courtroom, flanked by deputies judge Ito later told one veteran reporter ("off the record," of course) that he actually welcomed the woman's prayer. He described it as an "answer to prayer" because it offered one of the few positive spots to be seen in an otherwise soul-wrenching case. It is interesting to note that when the woman prayed, the feisty judge didn't use the gavel he had used so often before to censure offending journalists in the gallery for violations as minor as chewing gum during proceedings.

What was the story behind this seemingly bizarre incident? Was this just the outrageous act of another publicity- starved "wacko"? Was this woman a fanatic supporter of the defendant, O. J. Simpson, or just another "religious nut"? Was she a "juice profiteer" hoping to cash in on the media hype that had dogged the case ever since the infamous "Bronco run" over Los Angeles freeways? Is it true that she regularly prayed with Johnnie Cochran, Jr., and Robert Shapiro in front of sheriff's deputies and other defense team attorneys? The truth will surprise you, her background will shock you, and the reason for her actions may change your life forever. This is Tara Persaud's story of her unimaginable spiritual assignment as "intercessor" to what many observers have called "the trial of the century."

***

I suppose my story begins more than a quarter of a century ago in Guyana, a small nation bordering Venezuela to the east in South America. I decided to immigrate from Guyana to Canada in hopes of finding a better life and there married a Hindu man named Persaud. Things went reasonably well, and two years after my arrival in the city of Toronto and our subsequent marriage, our first daughter,

Shelley, was born in January of 1972. At the same time I converted to Roman Catholicism. Two years later, our second daughter, Roxanne, was born.

By January of 1993, the family was well established in Canada. After working for two Canadian banks and some private corporations, I had settled comfortably into a career position with Canada's Veterans Affairs office, and was enjoying success as a part-time real estate broker. My eldest daughter, Shelley, had experienced some ups and downs in a dating relationship, but was making plans to open her own retail paint and home decorating establishment with my help. Roxanne was about to finish her final year of high school, and things were looking good for the future. Then an inconceivable tragedy struck.

Shelley was working at a paint and wallpaper head office at the time, and we often talked about what she would need financially to open her own store. In the summer of 1992, Shelley confided to me that she had broken up with Patrick Deocharran, her boyfriend of two years. "I think he has a split personality, Mom," Shelley said. "I just don't want anything to do with him anymore." I thought of the times Patrick had attended church with me. I couldn't recall noticing any signs of mental problems or instability over the past two years, and I had even tried to help with some minor problems at one point. "He wants to get serious. In fact, he wants to marry me," Shelley said, "but I'm just not interested. He keeps switching personalities."

Despite that information, I couldn't help but feel a thrill of excitement as we made some definite plans for Shelley to open her dream store in the near future. She was very confident about her ability to run her own business. Beautiful and energetic, she was an outgoing person who was always eager to help and to please others, according to those who worked with her. These qualities had helped her excel at her job at the paint and wallpaper head office, and by January of 1993, she had purchased her first new car.

Unknown to me, Shelley had loaned Patrick $300 early in the summer of '92. When they broke up, Shelley told Patrick that she wanted the loan repaid. In retrospect, I don't think Shelley was really concerned about the money. I believe she just wanted to show Patrick that she was independent and didn't need his help or permission to move on in life.

Patrick evidently was using the $300 loan as a "string" to keep a direct line of contact with Shelley. About six months after their breakup, Shelley's 21'st birthday rolled around, and all her friends came to celebrate with her at a big birth- day party held two days later at our house on January 9, 1993. Patrick wasn't invited, and he didn't like it. I found out later from Shelley's friends that he actually showed up outside the house during the party and sent somebody inside with a message, asking her to come outside to talk with him. She refused to leave the house or meet him.

On February 1st, Patrick called Shelley at work and told her that he had the money he owed her. She left work at lunchtime and went to his house to pick up the money. He worked with heavy construction equipment, but was supposedly at home that week for some unknown reason. When Shelley arrived at his house, he didn't have the money after all, so she drove away and returned to her office. I still knew nothing about the $300 debt, or about Shelley's ongoing difficulties with Patrick.

On Thursday, February 4th, the Lord showed me a vision of my daughter's head going back in her car. It was lunchtime, and I had gone to lunch by myself. I decided to run back to the office to phone her, but I should have phoned her right then from the mall across the street. I felt I had to warn her to be careful, but I missed my opportunity. I came back to work within an hour of the vision and made my way directly to the phone. I quickly dialed the number for her office, but the person who answered the phone apologized and said Shelley had left just five minutes earlier. I had a sinking feeling, but I thought, *Maybe she is in danger of having a car accident or something,* and breathed a quick prayer.

All that afternoon, my spirit was troubled because of the vision I'd seen. I called a prayer line in Toronto to pray for her after I called her place of employment a half hour later, and then again an hour later, only to learn that she hadn't returned. I went back to my computer to do some work, and I suddenly heard Shelley crying out to me, "Mom! Mom!" After that, I just couldn't work anymore. I walked up and down the office floor, and at 2:30 p.m., I called her office again. She still wasn't there. At 3 o'clock I called again and my heart sank when I was told that she hadn't shown up, and no one had heard from her. That was when I told my coworkers I was leaving. Something was terribly wrong!

Before I left the office, I called Roxanne at school and told her to meet me at the house. When I walked into the house and triggered the answering machine, I had an emergency call from the hospital. When I called the hospital, I was told only that Shelley had "been in an accident." I said, "What kind of an accident?" thinking of my vision of her in the car. They said, "It involves a car, yes." Irritated by their vague replies, I pressed for an answer: "So Shelley is in the hospital. Now where is the car? Where was the accident?" In return, I was told, "The car is right here." I thought to myself, *that's strange.*

Meanwhile, my husband had felt that something was wrong too, so he too had left work early. He arrived home at the same time as Roxanne, and all three of us were preparing to leave for the hospital when the phone suddenly rang again. It was the hospital. The voice on the other end of the line said, "Mrs. Persaud, do you want someone from the police department to come for you?" In shock, I asked them, "Is my daughter dead or alive? Why do you want the police to take me to the hospital?" They said "No, she is in the operating room."

I quickly phoned my family members to tell them that Shelley had been in an accident and was in the hospital, and my brother-in-law came to pick us up and take us there. As we pulled out of our driveway, I heard the Lord tell me, "Shelley didn't make it through the operation," and I started to cry quietly in the van. Everyone asked, "Why are you crying?" I knew I had heard God's voice, and that was why I started to cry. He was preparing me for the worst even before I reached the hospital.

I told everyone in the van that Shelley had died, but they didn't want to accept it as fact. My husband went to pieces in grief; he was hoping that somehow his daughter would make it through this emergency that we knew so little about. We entered the doors of the hospital at 4:00 p.m., and we waited there without any contact from the doctors until 6:30 pm. when the surgeon came down.

The doctor told us that Shelley had died on the operating table. She went to be with the Lord at the exact time we were pulling out of the driveway of our home. The surgeon apologized and explained that he didn't come to see us earlier because he couldn't get himself together. Shelley's sudden death in the operating room had caught the entire operating room staff totally off guard. They had delayed Shelley's operation because she was talking to them right up until she went under the anesthesia.

Based on her clear brain function and vital signs, they thought she was going to make it through the surgery with no problems.

I discovered later that Patrick Deocharran had called Shelley at her office earlier in the day, and this time he swore that he had the money he owed her. Once again, Shelley left the office at lunchtime and drove to his house. As she pulled up at the curb, Patrick walked directly toward the passenger's side of her vehicle. Shelley thought he was holding the money he owed her, but he was actually hiding a long, sharp knife behind his back. Shelley's new car had power windows and power locks, but Patrick was in a rage. He literally broke the window on the passenger's side of the vehicle before she could drive away and savagely stabbed her four times in the chest. Miraculously, Shelley was still alive, and Patrick opened the driver's side door and moved her over into the passenger's seat. He was so obsessed with my daughter that he drove Shelley to the hospital in her own car, pulled up in the parking lot, and held her in his arms for a time as she continued to bleed externally and internally.

The police learned that Patrick actually made a bargain with Shelley while they were parked only a few yards from the Emergency Room entrance. He said, "If I take you into the hospital, I want you to tell them that somebody came and attacked the two of us." She was still talking at that point, and she agreed to the deal. Once the two entered the Emergency Room, the doctors rushed Shelley away into a private examination area and summoned the police, since she had obviously been stabbed. Once she was safely away from Patrick, my daughter told the medical staff about the "bargain" she'd been forced to agree to. She told them bluntly, "The truth is, *he did it.* He stabbed me four times, and he wants me to say that somebody else attacked us but nothing happened to him."

Shelley's funeral spanned four consecutive days as three different churches we were associated with came together for four services to accommodate the large crowds. The first funeral service was held the Saturday after her death, and the final service took place on Tuesday, February 9, 1993. In the end, nearly 500 souls were saved through the message of Christ delivered in each service-I knew Shelley would be pleased.

The funeral services took place in the middle of the Canadian winter, when the wind blows cold and virtually everything is frozen in Toronto. The chapel at the funeral home held about 1,000 people, and in each service, another 2,000 people stood outside the chapel in the cold listening as best as they could. Every night of the funeral services, the pastor made an altar call. The services were attended by masses of young people who were close to Shelley's age. She had attended nearby Bayview High School, and all the schools in the area had lowered their flags to half-mast in Shelley's honor. Somehow God had managed to turn the evil the devil had done into an incredible tool of His harvest.

After the funeral came the hard times—the lonely nights mourning her loss, the dread of treasured holidays and birthdays (both my husband and Roxanne celebrate their birthdays in February), and the difficult questions of "Why?" and "What could have been done to prevent Shelley's tragic murder?" Then there was Patrick Deocharran, the young man who had brutally murdered my daughter. I didn't realize it, but the grueling trials I would endure in the months ahead were destined to supernaturally prepare me for ministry in another country among other people who were embroiled in the sorrow, hatred, and anguish of the most publicized double murder case in modern history.

CHAPTER 2

Who Is OJ. Simpson?

The Persaud family was still reeling on a chilly Sunday evening in Toronto in June of 1994. They were struggling to regain their emotional footing after the brutal murder of Shelley Persaud 16 months before, and they weren't looking forward to the heartrending testimony they knew they would hear in the pretrial hearing for Shelley's accused murderer in September. Yet "the trial" constantly pressed its way into their thoughts and dreams.

Meanwhile, another drama was taking place that night in a posh West Los Angeles neighborhood 3,000 miles away. Nicole Brown Simpson and her friend, Ronald Goldman, were suddenly and violently confronted by a killer in the narrow confines of the entryway to Nicole's trendy condominium in Brentwood, California. The killer violently slashed his victims to death and quickly fled from the scene under cover of darkness on June 12, 1994.

When the victim's bloodstained dog finally led a neighbor to the murder scene shortly after midnight early Monday, June

13th, a 16-month ordeal hauntingly similar to that of the Persaud's began that would forever disrupt the lives of three bereaved families, and would rock the very foundations of law enforcement and judicial superstructures in the United States.

Ever since Shelley's final funeral service on February 9, 1993, I had continued to wrestle with the question, "Why did my daughter suddenly die on the operating table, even though the doctors thought she should have survived?" I immersed myself in God's presence and in His Word—He was my lifeline and source of strength through the most difficult months I have ever experienced.

Meanwhile, I watched my formerly happy family dissolve into a fractured collection of hurting, isolated individuals as each of us desperately tried to deal with our grief. I was miraculously sustained even in my deep pain, but I was deeply worried about Roxanne. She also tried to seek God for refuge, but she desperately missed her sister. She became too afraid to sleep alone, or even to be left alone during daylight hours for any length of time. My husband reacted the other way. He immediately withdrew in his grief, and avoided almost all contact with me as his anger toward "my Christian God" grew and intensified with each new day.

Only two months after Shelley's funeral, I received seven mysterious telephone calls at my home, all arriving within a half-hour period. Each time I answered the phone, I received no response. I could only hear a man sobbing almost uncontrollably on the other end of the line. Although the caller refused to speak, my suspicions were confirmed by the "Caller ID" feature on my telephone: My mystery caller was none other than Patrick Deocharran, the man accused of killing Shelley. I later learned that Patrick had just broken his bail agreement, instantly putting four of his family members in debt to the Canadian government for the equivalent of $20,000 each (the amount each had put up to secure Patrick's release from jail after his arrest in February). Although he had told the police he was not guilty, it was clear that guilt was rapidly eating away at his personality, and now he was on the run from the law. His bail was later revoked and he spent the next five months in jail awaiting the pretrial hearings and the trial itself.

In the midst of all the pain, questions, and stress, I couldn't let God go, and I refused to blame Him for Shelley's death because I knew it was the work of the devil, who is a thief and a murderer. As I continued to pray and seek God, He surprised me by telling me that He wanted to use me in courtrooms! I began to realize that God actually wanted me to pray in courthouses—I never dreamed that such a ministry existed. Thus when my friends had court cases, I began to take time off work to attend the court sessions and pray for them. Strangely enough, I could see that it was working.

The Holy Spirit began to tell me what was going to happen in these cases—*before* it took place in the courtroom. Each time, just as the Spirit told me, the attorneys would say or do exactly what I was told they would do. I just kept on praying. (It was the only thing I knew to do.) Just before the pretrial court hearing for my daughter's ex-boyfriend, God began to talk and minister to me in advance about what was going to happen in court. First He told me that Patrick would tell the truth to someone connected with the court, and admit what he did. I didn't know to whom or where this would take place, but I knew it would happen. I am convinced Patrick admitted to his attorney that he had murdered Shelley, but this was never admitted in court testimony or in any legal documents. He was convicted on the testimony of eyewitnesses and supporting evidence without a confession.

God also answered a question that was burning in my soul. At the end of August, 1994, the Lord showed me that Shelley had talked with Him about her earthly condition. He said that her injuries went beyond muscle and skeletal wounds to somehow involve her spinal cord. The doctors had been fooled because she talked so fluently and with such clarity of thought—but all the while her injuries were far more serious than they suspected. Her spinal cord injuries may have even blocked the pain that she should have felt, given the circumstances. Somehow Shelley knew that if she remained in this life, she would be paralyzed. God showed me that she had had a choice—she could stay and live on earth or go on to Heaven. She just didn't want to stay. Just knowing that Shelley had made that choice to leave somehow eased the terrible pain in my heart.

Meanwhile, Roxanne was taking Shelley's death very, very hard. I already mentioned that she didn't want to stay alone in the house by herself, so I had to make special arrangements during her final year in high school. Since at that time my husband went to work early, I asked my boss if I could come in at 9:00 am. and leave at 3:30 in the afternoon so Roxanne wouldn't be left alone. I am thankful for the way my boss at Canada's Department of Veterans Affairs supported me in those difficult times.

When Roxanne graduated from high school, we faced a new problem because she was left with even more time alone at home. She said, "Mom, I don't want to go to college because I can't really think about what I want to do right now. I would rather go to work. I want to look for a job." Since Roxanne didn't want to stay home and didn't have a job yet, I had to take her to work with me. Can you imagine what it was like for me to go to work with a 19-year-old child tagging along? Fortunately, the office had a computer lab where she could go and work on a computer and send out resumes. All day long she would work in that computer lab and then go home with me in the evening.

In the beginning, I shared with my husband the things God was showing me in prayer about Shelley, but he would have nothing to do with me or my God. When Shelley died, I think he lost all hope and turned his anger and resentment toward me and my faith in Christ. In his pain and bitterness, he even ordered me to stop going to church after the funeral was over. There was so much confusion and tension between us that we weren't even sleeping together, so Roxanne started sleeping with me in the guest room. It was a really crazy situation that was about to get worse.

I had to find my answers any way I could in those times with God—it was my way of dealing with the crushing grief and sense of loss. It didn't help when my husband stopped me from going to church, but his grieving had taken a dark and bitter turn. He didn't want to see a Bible or anything connected with the "Christian God." He refused to accept phone calls from anyone connected with a church or from my Christian friends. Finally, he demanded that Roxanne and I renounce our faith in Christ and return to Hinduism. (Roxanne was baptized and born again, and both of our daughters had attended Christian schools since they were five years old.)

I refused to turn away from Jesus Christ and embrace Hinduism as he demanded, and that became the root problem that destroyed our marriage. I was devouring the Bible and praying fervently for answers from God because He was my only salvation in the turmoil following Shelley's death. I earnestly looked to God for reassurance in my pain. I needed to know that He was real. (I'm trying to be honest with you rather than be "religiously correct")

At first I just went into the guest room to pray and read the Bible where it wouldn't bother my husband. But his growing intolerance for my faith and my unwillingness to turn to Hinduism finally took its toll, and I had to move into the guest room with Roxanne. Even then my husband would sometimes enter the room at night and wake me up just to demand, "Why are you reading the Bible?!" Then he would grab it and throw it on the floor, with his whole body shaking and trembling in anger. More than once after those late night confrontations I told the Lord, "Oh my God, I'm not going to touch Your Bible anymore." Yet each time, I had to return to His Word for survival. Then one night my husband dreamed that Shelley had returned to tell him, "You had better let Mom go back to church." After that, he told me I could go back to church, but still, something had permanently changed in our relationship.

The night before the pretrial hearing was to begin, Shelley appeared to me in a vision. She told me everything that happened and confirmed the things I'd learned from the Spirit of God about her injuries. Then she told me that she didn't want to come back and that we would have been grieved to see her bedridden and paralyzed for life.

I don't have an exhaustive theological explanation for Shelley's appearance to me more than a year after her death, but I remember that Jesus told His disciples about the rich man in Sheol who saw Abraham and Lazarus the beggar in Paradise. The rich man actually conversed with

Abraham, even though they were divided by a great gulf (see Lk. 16:22-26). In our case, both parties were washed in the blood of the Lamb of God, and the only gulf dividing us was the thin barrier between physical life and physical death, not the gulf between Heaven and hell. The Lord allowed Shelley to come; I didn't "call her up" as is practiced by those in the dark arts of the enemy. This only happened one time, and only in answer to prayer in Jesus' name requesting understanding. Finally, it came at a time of great need just before I was handed a humanly impossible task by the Lord Jesus Christ.

The next day at the pretrial hearing, I watched Shelley's former doctor take the witness stand while I thought, *I know what he is going to say, even before he says it.* Then the doctor followed the script God had already revealed to me in amazing detail. He testified under oath that Shelley's wounds would have definitely left her paralyzed had she survived, and I sat in that courtroom in amazement.

Throughout the preliminary hearing, I saw the hand of God at work showing me how to pray for both the prosecutor and the accused. In theory, the prosecutor was "on my side," but I had a strange mandate and grace from God to remain totally neutral-literally, I was on nobody's side! "How can that be? This hearing will determine what charges will be made against the man who murdered your own daughter-- how can you say you are on nobody's side?" I don't have a logical explanation for it. Even though I sat in that courtroom for two weeks listening to painful testimony about Shelley's death, I still felt sorry for the accused, and I didn't understand why. Then the Lord told me, "That is God's love. That is God's kind of love." Now, although I already knew what the doctor's testimony would reveal about Shelley's condition before her death, my husband had no idea of this. From the day we rushed to the hospital to the day of the hearing, he had sunk deeper and deeper into sorrow, anger, and bitterness. When he heard the doctor's testimony with all the gruesome details, he went to pieces emotionally and psychologically. The emotional stress of the preliminary hearing was so great for my husband that he reached a breaking point. Two weeks before the actual murder trial began in November, my husband moved out of our house to live with his sister, leaving Roxanne and I alone. He sat in on the trial proceedings, but he always went by himself, and my daughter and I always went together. I'm thankful that God's strength was so present in both my daughter and I through that ordeal.

It was during the preliminary hearings, on September 7, 1994, that the Lord also began to speak to me about someone named "O. J. Simpson." I had never heard of the man before, although I could remember hearing something about a double murder in California. I didn't know a thing about this stranger. Only later did I learn that he had been charged with killing his ex—wife and her male friend four months earlier. I really didn't care to find out, either. I was so busy concentrating on my own problems that I didn't watch TV or read much outside of God's Word. Yet in my prayer times, God persistently told me that He wanted me to cross the border and go to Los Angeles, California, to pray for participants in the O. J. Simpson trial.

I protested the assignment, and told the Lord, "I have never been to Los Angeles, or even to California, for that matter. And I don't know this man. I don't know anything about him. He is a stranger to me." I asked God, "Why would You want to send me there?" In the end, I knew it was the Lord telling me to go. Finally I said, "Yes, Lord, if I can get somebody to go with me, I will go. But I need somebody from Los Angeles, California, who knows the place. And Lord, could You send them to the Vineyard?" (I had begun to attend the Toronto Airport Vineyard Fellowship—now called the Toronto Airport Christian Fellowship—and was beginning to view it as my new "home church")

Not satisfied, I added, "Lord, somehow I think this man should be neither a black man nor a white man—he must be in between." Looking back on it, it sure sounds like I was making it rough on the Lord. I promised Him, "I will go if You will provide somebody who will go with me." He just told me to pray for that "someone," so I prayed throughout the month of October, and then I forgot about it.

After Patrick's murder trial ended in December, my husband told me he wanted a divorce. The divorce was granted in only two months—in the increasingly painful month of February. I didn't think that God could ever bring good out of this latest development, but in the end, it actually helped to prepare me to do His work.

Patrick's murder trial was marked by some bizarre incidents, and by the increased evidence of the grace of God in my life. Although I wanted justice to be done, for some reason I wasn't angry with Patrick for killing my daughter. This was God's grace in action. I know that sounds strange, but that was the way God positioned my heart and emotions. I was commissioned by God to pray for justice, and He helped me do so with neutrality.

As it turned out, there were witnesses to Shelley's murder, and after they testified under oath about what they had seen, a jury found Patrick guilty of second-degree murder after only four hours of deliberation (yet another odd parallel to the case just beginning to unfold in Los Angeles). He was sentenced to life in prison with the possibility of parole after ten years with good behavior. In the meantime, Patrick messed up again while in jail during the trial.

Patrick was caught plotting to kill one of the witnesses in his case with the help of another murder suspect in jail. When the second plotter shared the scheme with a third inmate, that person reported it to the authorities. (Even prison felons have no use for individuals who commit certain "crimes without honor.") The police planted an undercover cop in Patrick's cell, and sure enough, he approached the undercover agent with a scheme to kill the same witness, and was arrested on charges of "conspiracy and counselling a 'hit man' to commit murder." Patrick pleaded guilty to the lesser charge of "counselling to commit the offense of attempting to obstruct justice" and was sentenced to two more years in prison, which delayed for 12 years the possibility of parole while serving his life sentence.

I prayed through all the proceedings in the murder case, and each time I heard a witness testify about the death of my precious daughter, I became more and more angry with Satan. I blamed him for it all, not God. Satan had come to steal my marriage, my family, and my oldest daughter. Now I had a divine mandate to "get him back" through the power of Jesus' cross, blood, and name. I also was commanded to teach others how to "do battle" and destroy the works of the enemy through the name of Jesus Christ. I just had no idea where that mandate would lead me in the following months and years.

CHAPTER 3

Destination: The City of Angels

The city of Toronto was once again shivering in the arctic winds of a frigid Canadian winter when North American television viewers from Montreal, Quebec, to Key West, Florida, were transfixed by the testimony of Denise Brown, the older sister of Nicole Brown Simpson, the slain ex-wife of 0. J. Simpson.

In an emotion-charged testimony often interrupted by sobs and tears, Ms. Brown described scenes in which Simpson had publicly humiliated his wife, and hurled her against a wall in their home in a fit of anger. These vivid images of the dark side of a revered American sports and movie hero shocked the nation on February 3, 1995—only one day before the second anniversary of Shelley Persaud's murder. Despite defense objections during the preliminary hearing, the prosecution was permitted to admit evidence of Simpson's acts of domestic violence as part of the case. Three months earlier, the jury had been selected and then sequestered for what was quickly dubbed "The 0. J. Trial." In January, the two leading black attorneys on opposing sides in the case clashed over national television while debating "the role of race" in the trial. Defense attorney Johnnie Cochran, Jr., was once a mentor to prosecutor Christopher

Darden, but on January 13th, they locked horns in an emotional argument centered around the right of the O. J. Simpson defense team to question Detective Mark Fuhrman about his alleged racial slurs. Darden pleaded with judge ho to forbid the use of "the n-word" by defense attorneys, saying, "It is the dirtiest, filthiest, nastiest word in the English language." He went on to argue that it would pressure the jurors to choose between "the white prosecutors and the white policemen" and the "black defendant and his very prominent and capable black lawyer."

After Darden's statements, many observers felt that defense attorney Johnnie Cochran, Jr., began to "taunt" Darden by reading aloud from documents quoting Fuhrman using "the n—word." He claimed Darden was insulting the jury because "African-Americans live with offensive words... every day. . . and yet they still believe in this country."

Seven days later, Judge Daniel Ito ruled that the defense could allege racism as a motive for Detective Fuhrman's actions if they could prove it was relevant to the case. The public was shocked again by yet another revelation of alleged racism in one of the largest law enforcement organizations in the world—an organization already under fire for its misconduct in the arrest and unlawful beating of Rodney King. Already it was apparent that the looming racial and social issues outside of the case threatened to overshadow the actual fact-finding mission of the court. Many observers felt a mistrial was in the making.

The first prosecution witness was a 911 operator who testified she answered a call from the Simpson home on New Year's Day in 1989. Millions of viewers recoiled at the terror depicted when the unedited audio recording of Nicole Brown Simpson's plea for protection from her husband was played That recording would be replayed hundreds of times before the conclusion of the trial 16 long months later—with the most dramatic replay occurring in Marcia Clark's final summation before the jury was adjourned to deliberate on a verdict.

February of 1995 was a dark month marked by dramatic life transitions for my family. Shelley's murder trial ended with Patrick Deocharran's conviction for second degree murder and sentencing in December, followed by a pain-filled and empty Christmas holiday. Thirteen days later I struggled through what would have been Shelley's 23rd birthday, and I had to help Roxanne to somehow get through her own birthday on February 26th. Everything was overshadowed by the second anniversary of Shelley's death on February 4, 1995.

My estranged husband's birthday came on February 9th, and his absence from our home and lives was a painful and brooding reality we couldn't ignore. His absence was made official and permanent with a judge's decree of divorce on February 21, 1995. I had lost a daughter, a husband, a marriage, and the family life in which I had invested nearly two decades of my existence. Roxanne lost her older sister and best friend, and was deprived of her father's continual presence in her life. Now she was facing the loss of the security she had enjoyed since birth.

The events and painful memories of February, 1995 again threw our emotions into upheaval. At times it seemed impossible to go on. (My heart goes out to the Brown and Goldman families, and to the Simpson children, whose pain will always be especially felt on certain days of the calendar, a pain heightened by special memories of their slain loved ones that will force their way to the surface every holiday and special family occasion.)

In the midst of this turmoil, God was still speaking to my heart about "the call" to pray for the "O. J. trial." I committed myself to obey, but managed to busy myself with other things in the meantime. I put my house up for sale, and I planned to split the proceeds with my ex-husband. When the house didn't sell right away, I decided to rent it. Another real estate agent brought in a tenant and I signed a rental contract on it. Somehow I just didn't want to stay there any longer, and my ex—husband was still living with his sister. When I sent the contract to him, he didn't want to sign it. He wanted me to either sell the house outright and give him his money, or stay in the house myself (so he would still have a way to control or keep contact with me).

In desperation I asked the Lord, "Do You want me to go back and forth from Toronto to Los Angeles on this 0. J. case? Well, I have to find a place to live, and I have to find that man to help me in that big city, and I need to get the contract signed by my ex-husband so my tenant can move in." That is when He told me, "Check the tenant's credit. He does not have good credit, and that will release you from the contract."

When I did what the Lord told me to do, I discovered that the tenant had a bad credit rating! As soon as I dissolved that rental contract, I had another offer from a prospective rental tenant. Again my ex-husband refused to sign the rental agreement, claiming that he would stay in the house. He was especially irritated by my intention to travel to California for the 0. J. trial. All he could see were the lost sales opportunities on the days I was out of the house and out of town.

One time I went to Chicago for a weeklong "spiritual warfare" conference with Morris Cerullo. That made my ex-husband furious because I wasn't home that week to show the house to prospective buyers. He said, "I want my money!" and started to threaten me, saying he was going to kill me for the money! It was clear to me that Satan was trying to attack me by stirring up my ex—husband. I was especially alarmed by his threat to kill me. The spirit inspiring those words bore a striking resemblance to the spirit that inspired my daughter's killer. (As of this writing, the house has been sold and I plan to pay my ex-husband his part of the sales proceeds. I am also praying that this spirit of anger and murder doesn't stay on him.)

On March 15th, I attended a conference held at the Toronto Airport Vineyard Fellowship on "The Word of God and Spiritual Strongholds." My schedule was busy, but somehow I felt it was vital that I attend this conference. I had no idea just how vital it was until later on. I should have known something important was going on when I became severely ill with a high fever for three days the week before the conference. During those difficult days in my home, the Lord often talked to me about the task ahead. I even received a visitation from the angel Gabriel who shared a few more pieces to the puzzle of this task with the O. J. Simpson case.[1] (God didn't tell me the whole story. He just led me one day at a time.) On Wednesday, the first day of the conference, I joined in a conversation with a man wearing a clerical collar and a woman who was talking about intercessory prayer. Shortly after I joined them, the woman was drawn away for some reason, and I continued my conversation with the clergyman, an associate minister named Lewis Smith from Carter's Temple AME Church in Chicago. I told him about

1 I realize that this may sound a bit far—fetched to many readers, but it seemed perfectly natural to me. Perhaps the years I spent in the Roman Catholic Church made me more willing to accept such an active role by an angelic messenger. In any case, this visitation was very real to me, and the angel's role was primarily to support and confirm the leading I had already received in prayer to God. I suspect that God uses angels in our lives more often than most of us realize that the man was interested in me as a romantic interest, and I didn't "want a man." (I was extremely sensitive about the issue because I had just been an unwilling participant in a divorce and was still recovering from the trauma of losing my oldest daughter.)

the strong burden I had for the judicial system, and I told him I wasn't happy. I think he was a bit surprised by my statement, but I told him that I just couldn't do what God wanted me to do without some help. For some reason, I didn't tell him about my daughter's murder, or about God's call to pray for the "O. J. Simpson trial." (You just don't go around telling everybody about something like that.) I halfway suspected

***

I will never forget the first conversation I had with Tara Persaud. We met in the course of a three-way conversation at a conference sponsored by what was then called the Toronto Airport Vineyard Fellowship. The morning meeting had been dismissed and most of the people had already left the lobby to go to lunch in nearby restaurants. When the third party in our conversation left, I turned to Tara and asked, "What kind of ministry has Jesus called you into?" Her answer caught me off guard: "A big one, Reverend Smith. Jesus has called me into a weird ministry." I just had to find out more. "Did I hear you say 'a weird ministry'? If that's the case, why don't we go out for lunch so you can tell me more about it?"

That first fascinating interchange naturally led to more questions over lunch. I realized that I was a stranger to this woman, and I somehow sensed that she was uneasy about something. Yet the more she talked about her call, the more animated and enthusiastic she became. As she began to describe the way God had called her to win souls and to enter in courtrooms through prayer, I found that my interest level kept going up. I was especially fascinated with the way God spoke to her about future events in various trial proceedings, and with her commitment to remain "neutral" in her prayer function in courtroom situations. I had never heard of another ministry like hers. After lunch, we parted ways with the usual "see you tomorrow" statements, but I was even more aware of the coolness I sensed toward the end of the lunch. Mrs. Persaud was noticeably uneasy and I figured it had to do with the "man-woman" thing, so I decided to just back off and give her the space she needed just the same, there was something supernatural about her that was hard to ignore.

Later on Tara told me that when she went home that day, the Lord started talking to her about me. He said, "You only told that man half the story. You need to tell him the *whole story.*" Tara reacted defensively, revealing exactly where her heart—and her fears—were: "Lord, I don't want the man. I don't need a man. I don't even remember the man's name." Then God reminded her of the prayer she offered in October of 1994 asking for a helper, a man who could help her fulfill her mission in Los Angeles. "No, no, no," the Lord said. "This man is going to be working with you." So that is how she knew (before I did) that God had sent me to Toronto specifically to meet her.

The next day of the conference, I didn't realize it, but Tara was actively looking for me. When she found me, I followed through with my earlier decision to stay cool and give her space. Unfortunately, what came across to her was, "Oh, this time he just isn't impressed." Yet Tara persisted and asked me to go to lunch with her again. I thought to myself, *why should I talk to her at lunch?* But I finally gave in and said, "Okay, at lunchtime I will talk to you." I have to admit that I was puzzled by the change in Tara's attitude toward me and my interest in her ministry. I wasn't sure what would take place over lunch, but I was confident that it would definitely be "different." After all, I was having lunch for a second time with a woman called to "a weird ministry."

***

I sat across the table from Rev. Smith that Thursday afternoon and told him "the whole story" of my daughter's violent death, my subsequent divorce, and my calling and appointment as intercessor to the "O. J. trial." I even told him about the prayer for a male "helper" I had offered to God so many months ago. It felt strange to share such private hurts and "outlandish" revelations with a stranger-and a man no less—but then I heard a voice down in my spirit say to me, "I want you to buy this man a plane ticket to Los Angeles." I could sense this was the voice of the Lord Jesus, so I swallowed hard and asked Rev. Smith if he would be interested in the "assignment." He said, "I will do what the Lord says. If He says so—and I think He has—then I'll do it." I was shocked when Rev. Smith agreed with the word I had received from the Lord, but then he added, "I think I'm supposed to do this for you, Mrs. Persaud. But I have to inform my pastor and the leadership at the church that sent me here for this special conference."

We then went directly to the Toronto Airport to make flight arrangements, for we both sensed that the time to act was right then. Although Rev. Smith already had airline tickets for the return flight to Chicago, we had to make arrangements to get him from Chicago to Los Angeles. Later I found out that even though Rev. Smith had come from Chicago where he was an associate minister at one of the city's largest churches, he also had more than ten years of solid ministry experience in the city of Los Angeles. He also was of mixed racial descent. These were just other confirmations that Jesus had led the right person into my pathway to help me fulfill the calling He had placed upon my life.

I had another surprise in store for me that afternoon. When the Lord told me to buy Rev. Smith a ticket to fly to Los Angeles, I thought the tickets would cost around $400. I was shocked to discover they would cost me $1,000! All of a sudden, my level of commitment would have to "double." Once again, I swallowed hard and paid for the tickets. Rev. Smith didn't even stay on for the conclusion of the conference—he boarded a plane for Chicago that same day, determined to share his new assignment with his pastor.

I knew in my heart when Tara shared about her ministry that my life was destined to be intertwined with her mission. I also knew it would cost me something. I had been an international evangelist associated with Morris Cerullo World Evangelism Ministries in San Diego, California, for more than 15 years. I had traveled extensively through the United States and Canada teaching soul-winning and conducting revival services. In recent years, I had become deeply involved in teaching pastors how to teach their people soul-winning. I was doing this kind of work in Chicago when I met Pastor Williamson of Carter's Temple, the largest AME church in Chicago. He saw that I was gifted in the areas of soul-winning and church growth, so he asked me to join his staff as associate pastor. He had a vision to increase the size of the flock there from 1,500 to 5,000 believers, and he wanted to do it the "old-fashioned way" by winning the lost to Jesus. That is why he sent me to Toronto. Originally we had planned to attend the conference together, but he was so busy that I had to go to the conference alone. I knew the day I sat at that restaurant table with Tara that I could only handle one major assignment at a time, and the choice had just been made for me by the Holy Spirit.

During the flight back to Chicago, I thought about Pastor Williamson and his dream to see a greater church built for God in Chicago. Was his vision from God? Absolutely. Was he wrong to ask me to help him bring the vision to pass? No. Yet now I would have to tell this respected man of God that God had reassigned me to another task. As I had anticipated on the plane, Pastor Williamson wasn't exactly thrilled with my news. Although he is always happy to see God's Kingdom built and the name of Jesus glorified, he was definitely struggling with my latest bit of news. To his credit, he told me, "Okay, if God is telling you to do this, and you are sure of it, then He will take care of you." I left there wishing the best for the local body and Pastor Williamson, but an obvious by-product of the pastor's answer was that there would be no financial support coming from the local body there to help me in this new assignment. It wasn't easy to leave such an excellent ministry opportunity behind. Nevertheless, I was determined to pursue the new direction God had set before me—knowing that I had just cut off my primary source of income and ministerial support for the sake of this new call (and little else).

Tara made arrangements to pick up a complete set of tapes from the conference and sent the set on to Pastor Williamson and the church body in Chicago, since the church had sent me to Toronto for that exact reason. Once that was taken care of, I was free to focus on the details of my new calling.

This latest adventure was made even more difficult by the fact that my new role in this "calling" was to be "Number 2." God had assigned me to be a covering and a support to a woman He had sovereignly called and equipped for a difficult work I was able to take the assignment only because the Spirit of God allowed me to pick up a measure of the seriousness of the assignment. (At the time, neither one of us really knew just how serious and how far-reaching this assignment would be.) The second difficulty dealt with finances. For reasons known only to God, when He assigned Tara to pray for the 0. J. trial, He also made it clear that she was to "foot the bill" for the expenses of the ministry—including my expenses. Any man, who has grown used to working hard, paying his own bills, and providing for others, knows just how hard it is to let someone else take over the financial responsibility of paying expenses. That was one of the hardest challenges I faced in this assignment. In the end, Tara personally invested more than $40,000 in this assignment to cover our travel, hotel, and dining expenses.

I was able to defray a portion of my expenses because a number of churches in the Los Angeles area had already scheduled me to come and minister to their congregations that spring and summer, and all but one of those meetings worked out fine. When that particular weeklong service went so well that I was asked to continue for another week, I was faced with a choice after I received an urgent call from Tara in which she told me she would arrive on the same date as the extended ministry booking. I had to go with my highest priority—the support and care of Tara Persaud as she ministered to the court in Los Angeles.

There is a biblical precedent for such an arrangement in the lives and ministry of Deborah and Barak in judges 4:4-14. Deborah the prophetess was a judge over Israel at the time. She was the one who sat under "the palm tree of Deborah" and judged the matters and disagreements of the Israelite people. Barak was a man she selected at the leading of the Spirit of God to help her bring down Sisera, the most deadly enemy of Israel at the time. They rose up and went to battle together, but ironically, Deborah prophesied (accurately) that Sisera would fall "at the hand of a woman" in the end, not by the armed might or skill of Barak. As for the financial situation, even a casual reading of the Gospels in the Bible indicates that much of the ministry of Jesus Christ was underwritten by wealthy women who fervently believed in the Lord's mission.

The Holy Spirit spoke to me and said, "I have chosen you to cover Tara Persaud. No matter who lets her down, don't *you* ever let her down." So I made that exact commitment to her. I promised Tara, "No matter what happens, I Will never let you down," and she took me at my word. Any time she needed anything concerning the OJ. Simpson case, she called on me.

The first thing that God told Tara to do was pray for Johnnie Cochran, Jr., and Robert Shapiro, the lead attorneys for O. J. Simpson. From the beginning, we knew these assignments from

God had nothing to do with Simpson's innocence or guilt, or with one side winning over the other. We had been dispatched as strictly neutral participants. We were there in God's interests, and His interests alone. With that first assignment in mind, on Monday morning March 20th, I boarded a jet and flew directly from Chicago to Los Angeles to find a good base of operations in a local hotel. I wanted to find every key location at the Criminal Courts Building in downtown Los Angeles, including "Department 103," the official name of the courtroom where Superior Court judge Lance Ito was presiding over the unfolding 0. J. Simpson trial.

I knew going into this that we needed supernatural favor to accomplish our task. When I landed in Los Angeles, God gave me faith to accomplish the job. Even before I made the trip, I felt strongly that I was to wear a clerical collar throughout the assignment so the many kinds of people we would encounter would know who Tara and I were representing at the trial. The wisdom of this decision became clear almost from the beginning.

CHAPTER 4

Divine Appointment at the Elevator

The day Tara Persaud first met Rev. Lewis Smith in Toronto, Canada, Detective Mark Fuhrman responded to fierce cross-examination by defense attorneys in Los Angeles, California, denying under oath before the jury that he had used the infamous "n-word" as a racial slur over the past ten years. Prosecutors hoped to blunt the growing backlash of public Opinion against Fuhrman and the Los Angeles Police Department (and the majority of the state's evidence that his investigative work had provided). Fuhrman's denial followed three days of testimony by his partner, Detective Philip Vannatter, who publicly acknowledged misstatements and questionable handling of evidence in the case. Legal experts around the country agreed that the proceedings were in grave danger of being dismissed and a mistrial judgment delivered.

The racial implications of the case were exploding out of control, threatening to engulf the already volatile greater Los Angeles community. (The situation wasn't helped when it was later proven that Detective Fuhrman had indeed used the racial slur over the past decade—including 42 times in a hate filled interview with a screenwriter recorded on audiotape! Fuhrman invoked the Fifth Amendment when challenged about the truthfulness of his earlier testimony in court proceedings conducted apart from the jury, barely avoiding criminal prosecution for perjury.)

The jury had been under severe sequestration for nearly three months by the time Brian "Kato" Kaelin, a man described by the media as "the mop-headed man known as America's most famous houseguest" testified that he was the last person to see his host, 0. J. Simpson, on the night of the murders. Yet even "Kato" Kaelin's testimony seemingly didn't account for the "crucial hour" during which 0. J. Simpson allegedly murdered Nicole Brown Simpson and Ron Goldman.

The greatest blow to the defense to date came on Monday, March 27th, when the prosecution introduced compelling testimony by expert Witnesses who stated that the blood samples taken at the crime scene, from 0. J. Simpson's infamous white Ford Bronco, and at his home several miles away from Nicole's condominium, indicated that 0. J. Simpson "could not be ruled out" as a suspect in the double slayings.

The jury and those sitting in the courtroom were shocked by seven-foot tall full-color photographs of the severely slashed bodies of the victims at the crime scene. The proceedings were dismissed early after some jurors were sickened by the graphic images of violence and sudden death. (Television camera feeds were cut, and all news photography was banned due to the gruesome nature of the photographs.) Legal experts around the country told television audiences that the prosecution's case was gaining tremendous strength despite the initial negative impact of the Fuhrman controversy.

***

My first week back in Los Angeles, I chose the Ramada Inn on Century Boulevard as our base of operations. It is just a short 20 minutes away from the Criminal Courts Building in Los Angeles via Broadway and the downtown expressway. Each time Tara Persaud came to Los Angeles, I reserved the same two rooms side by side. After the first visit, the staff knew us personally and began to go out of their way to take care of our needs over the next few months.

From my first day "on the job" to the day the verdict was delivered, I always wore my clerical collar in public to clearly identify my "boss" (God) and to give some indications about my motives for being on the scene of the O. J. Simpson case. A side benefit that I hadn't considered was that it made me stick out in a crowd—a fact that became apparent when reporters and various visitors began to seek me for interviews and counsel week after week. In contrast to the wide assortment of onlookers, performers, sales representatives, hecklers, and outright clowns, I must have seemed pretty mild to those who saw me.

The first day I visited the courthouse site, I discovered that "Department 103" (the name of the Superior courtroom where the trial proceedings for the Simpson case took place) was located on the ninth floor of the Criminal Courts Building. That floor was specially designed and reserved for trials requiring special security. Unlike larger courtrooms elsewhere in the building, "Department 103" had only 80 seats in its gallery for spectators, and it featured a bulletproof enclosure for an armed guard who remained on duty during all court proceedings. I also learned that the entire ninth floor had been sealed off from the general public, and access was only granted by elevator to the few spectators and media representatives who were selected for the available seats each day. Everyone else had to wait in the first floor lobby outside the courthouse building.

Everything looked rather grim until I met a news photographer named George Redy. He had the run of the whole courthouse, with access to all the different floors. God gave me supernatural favor with George from that first day on. (In fact, he invited me to stay in his home for a time during a period when Tara remained in Canada.) When he went into the courthouse and walked past the security guards, they instantly recognized him as a credentialed news photographer. That automatically got me in because I "was with him." God used George to introduce me to scores of key television news people covering the trial. George also took me up to the media room on the twelfth floor, which was set aside for the hundreds of print and broadcast journalists who couldn't get into the courtroom. Tara and I were granted access to the room and other restricted areas virtually anytime we were there on assignment. It was equipped with an audio feed of the trial proceedings and 250 phone lines. I believe some of the electronic media outlets set up their control centers there as well. The largest collection of television and radio equipment, however, was set up across the street from the courthouse in a lot dubbed "Camp O. J" and was serviced by 650 outgoing telephone and communication lines.

By the end of the first week, I knew I was ready for Tara's arrival. Despite all the preparations I'd made, however, I knew from my on-site investigation and by the Spirit that Tara Persaud would have absolutely no success in her mission apart from the supernatural intervention and provision of God. It was totally in His hands.

***

I was praying for Rev. Lewis from the moment he left for Chicago to the day I met him at the airport in Los Angeles a week or so later. The whole time while I was in Toronto, I was undergoing tremendous spiritual attack. We talked on the telephone each day, and I remember telling him how my hands and feet just throbbed with pain each time I finished praying for him and the tasks he faced each day. By the grace of God, he had everything in place by the time I arrived in Los Angeles on Sunday, March 26th. I knew when I walked into the Ramada Inn on Century Boulevard that it was the place the Lord wanted us to be for this assignment.

I will never forget my first morning in Los Angeles. I was getting ready for my first visit to the courthouse where the 0. J. Simpson case was being tried, and just before Rev. Smith came to pick me up, I had a surprise visit from Satan himself! He appeared in my room and told me, "I am Lucifer, and I am going to take you off this case." I responded to Satan (it didn't matter to me that he stilled called himself by his "pre-fall" name of Lucifer—he's just the devil to me), "*You did not assign me to this case, and in Jesus' name, you are not going to take me off it!*" The "battle" was on from that time on.

When we arrived at the Criminal Courts Building, I immediately understood why news commentators and columnists were calling the scene around the trial "a circus." You would be hard—pressed to find a stranger combination of characters, activities, opinions, and tensions that were gathered outside the courthouse on a daily basis for almost a year and a half!

The security precautions were extensive and highly visible near the courthouse and especially in the lobby area. Although I knew Rev. Smith had enjoyed some success in his preparation work, I still wasn't prepared for the kind of favor we encountered that morning. Rev. Smith introduced me to his friend, George

Redy, and then those two led me past the watching battery of guards like they owned the place.

Rev. Smith explained that the attorneys on the defense team always used the freight elevators in a restricted part of the courthouse to make their way up to the Superior courtroom on the ninth floor. No one else was allowed back there except for assigned sheriff's deputies stationed at the elevator door and us! He also told me that the district attorney's team came in through another way in another part of the building, so we wouldn't have such easy access to those attorneys. I was disappointed, but determined to trust God in that area. We came to Los Angeles with a mandate to be neutral in the case, and that meant that the prosecution needed and deserved our prayer support as much as the defense. We never veered from that mandate.

On my first day at the courthouse, I found myself standing with Rev. Smith and George Redy beside the freight elevators in the bowels of the Criminal Courts Building, waiting for the defense attorneys to arrive. Our only company was the guard detail from the sheriff's office. They already seemed to know Rev. Smith by name. I sensed that they were extremely curious about us and what we would do in the next half hour. They were about to find out (along with us).

We heard a stir outside and a call came in over the walkie-talkies warning the deputies that the defense attorneys had arrived and were wading through the massed army of media representatives and onlookers. Evidently O. J. Simpson was always taken to a special holding area in the building first, and the attorneys proceeded to the elevators after remanding their client to the custody of sheriff's deputies. I watched the hallway intently, while praying softly for opportunity and wisdom. I was to receive both that very morning.

My first encounter with Johnnie Cochran, Jr., and Robert Shapiro was totally orchestrated by the Lord, as I knew it would be. The two leading attorneys on 0. J. Simpson's so-called "Dream Team" were nearly neck and neck as they led an entourage toward the same freight elevator they had used for nearly seven months. But something different was going to happen today. I had prayed that God would do something to show them that He alone was controlling this case-not man. He had priorities and purposes that ranged far beyond the walls of that courtroom.

When I stepped forward and asked the attorneys if I could pray for them, they meekly agreed and allowed me to pray a brief prayer that God would have His way that day. I didn't pray that they, or their opponents, would win or lose—I simply prayed that God's will would be done. George Redy was dumbstruck by the fact that these high-powered attorneys nationally known for their aggressive verbal combat skills and the ability to dominate conversations and situations would so willingly subject themselves to our ministry.

After the prayer, Cochran and Shapiro politely thanked me for the prayer and moved quickly onto the freight elevator, followed by their entourage of attorneys, deputies, and support people. As soon as the elevator doors closed, Rev. Smith and I looked at each other and shook our heads in wonder. Only God could work the kind of miracle we had just experienced. Meanwhile, outside the courthouse were thousands of reporters, commentators, and onlookers who would do almost anything to reach the men we had just prayed for.

Beginning at nine o'clock that morning, the defense team experienced perhaps their toughest day on trial since the case was begun. The media quickly spread the news about the dramatic results of initial blood analysis tests and the graphic full-color, bigger-than-life photos of the slashed murder victims that were repeatedly displayed before shocked and sickened jurors. God knew the prosecution would have days that were just as bad, and in the end, the ragged edge of human conduct and eroding values would be revealed in some of America's most elite and revered institutions. Yes, if there was ever a case where God should have His way, this was it. Regardless of the verdict, the United States would never be the same.

We also went to the courthouse on Tuesday and Wednesday, although I never felt led to go seek a pass to enter the courtroom itself. I had already been assured in prayer that the time for that would come later. Most of the time I remained in the lobby area or spent time up in the restricted media room on the twelfth floor. My central assignment was to pray, and I tried to stay focused on my mission, not on all the distractions swirling around the trial. I quickly realized that God always had a reason when He prompted me to leave Toronto to pray from the physical location of the trial. Thus, I was also responsible to remain sensitive to the leading and promptings of the Holy Spirit when I was at the courthouse.

The Spirit often led me to key people who needed prayer, or led me to intervene in emergency situations in the spirit realm. I realize this may sound "spooky," but it isn't. The primary forces driving both the crime and the trial were rooted in the spirit realm. God had called me and Rev. Smith to be part of the team to bring His purposes to pass through obedience.

On Wednesday, George Redy (who is African-American) introduced Rev. Smith and I to Johnnie Cochran, Jr.'s wife and O. J. Simpson's sisters as they had lunch with Mr. Cochran in the courthouse lunchroom. They graciously allowed us to pray for them, and I learned that Johnnie Cochran, Jr.'s wife is a strong Christian. (I also discovered that her husband was a deacon in a Baptist church, although he wasn't born again at that point; and confirmed that Robert Shapiro was Jewish.)

From the beginning, the OJ. Simpson trial was marked by an ominous threat of racial strife, misunderstanding, and emotional chaos that could engulf the entire nation. As I began to pray for the case, the Lord made it clear to me that He was about to uncover the hidden seeds of destruction that had been carefully concealed and buried by major institutions in the United States. He was doing this to treat a cancer that would surely destroy the nation if it was not discovered, admitted, uprooted, and destroyed. As I shared my insights with Rev. Smith, he began to share some racial incidents in the Bible that totally confirmed what I had picked up by the Spirit in prayer.

The world gets darker by the day, while the Church of Jesus Christ, called to be light and salt to the world, is failing to meet the challenge and fulfill her role to implement change in our society. Without her spiritual light and salt, our entire world will continue to deteriorate. One of the major problems plaguing the Church itself is the problem of racism. I classify racism as a "skin disease" because it is the spiritual and social equivalent of "leprosy" in any church, community, or nation.

In ancient times, and even in areas plagued by this disease today, those who contract leprosy are segregated, isolated, and gradually weakened and debilitated by this affliction. Although it manifests in the skin, it is caused by a tiny bacteria that attacks the nervous system, killing every sensitivity toward pain, injury, and removing all natural feeling and sensation from the victim's stricken area. Entire segments of our society are being isolated by their racial leprosy. Their behavior and standards of life are being degraded as their sensitivity and natural senses are stripped from them. They are losing the ability to feel the injury they have inflicted on people of other color, though they will quickly accept the life-giving red blood from their veins should they face a life-threatening injury in an emergency room.

The Church cannot fulfill her calling without addressing the issue of racism *publicly*. The same is true of the nation. Racism cannot be swept under the carpet. It has infiltrated and contaminated the highest levels of government, law enforcement, and education, and of the Church herself. It must be squarely addressed if it is to be controlled and then eliminated. For a Church called to be peculiar and different "in the midst of a crooked and perverse nation, among whom ye shine as lights in the world" (Phil. 2:15b), compromise with leprosy is no longer acceptable.

Countless numbers of Christians and Christian leaders are suffering from a chronic and potentially fatal "skin problem," yet they insist on trying to keep that disease while still living as a member of the Body of Christ. The only way to live this way is to ignore and defy the direct command of Jesus Christ, who said:

> *"And if thy right eye offend thee, pluck it out, and cast it from thee: for it is profitable for thee that one of thy members should perish, and not that thy whole body should be cast into hell. And if thy right hand offend thee, cut it out and cast it from thee: for it is profitable for thee that one of thy members should perish, and not that thy whole body should be cast into hell* (Matthew 5:29-30)."

You do not need the right skin to enter Heaven; you need the right spirit! The Church throughout the world has been earnestly praying and waiting for the revival that God promised to bring before the return of Jesus Christ on earth. So far, nothing spectacular has happened. If prayer alone were to bring revival, by now it would have happened. What then is the problem? *Love always precedes revival!*

In the Book of Acts, when the apostles noticed racial discrimination in the Church, they dealt with it right away. They made sure that all were treated equally without preference, and their actions brought stability and unity to the Body of Christ. All parties were pleased by the actions they took. They didn't consider Greek believers to be inferior to Jewish believers. Even in the appointment of deacons over the affairs of the Church, they made sure that both Greeks and Jews were fairly represented. By making way for love to flow in the Body of Christ, they paved the way for the Word of God to increase, and then the number of disciples multiplied greatly in Jerusalem. Great signs and wonders followed their evangelistic ministry. It was love that brought revival in the early ministry of the apostles.

One of the most serious challenges to the early Church in her first 25 years or so was racism. Although the apostle Peter had received a direct revelation from God about the equality of all races in Acts 10, he succumbed to peer pressure from other Jewish believers and showed favoritism. Paul the apostle couldn't stand by and allow this aberration from God's clear command to go unchallenged, so he publicly rebuked Peter and again restored obedience to God's commands concerning racial equality in the Church (see Gal. 2:11-14). God still demands racial equality and total love toward others in our churches, our schools, our educational institutions, and in our government. This is why the Lord spoke to me and said, "One of the greatest problems preventing revival is racism."

Racism is a platform for hate, and it is a disease that should have no place among Christians. Who are we to despise anyone who is made in the image of God, the Creator? If God Almighty openly chooses to dwell in people of all colors, then who are we to refuse to fellowship with the same people?

CHAPTER 5

Facing the Cross in the Courtroom

The month of April, 1995, brought storm clouds of renewed racial tension and strife to the small Superior courtroom on the ninth floor of the Criminal Courts Building on Temple Street in the heart of Los Angeles, California. Another judicial "first" was racked up when the jury refused to be seated in the jury panel in a rebellion unprecedented in American jurisprudence. That was followed by public outrage among members of the Asian community over a renowned defense attorney's disparaging "off-the-record" remarks about Dennis Fung, a Los Angeles Police Department criminologist. In all the furor, the crime against the victims and the goal of justice for the accused somehow seemed to get lost.

First, Judge Ito was forced to suspend testimony in the case when 13 of the 18 jurors and alternates showed up outside the courtroom dressed in black to protest the judge's abrupt removal of three sheriff's deputy-bailiffs assigned to see to the needs of the jurors. The deputies were removed after a juror who had been dismissed from the panel earlier accused the deputies of favoring white jurors over black jurors. The 13 protestors were black, white, and Hispanic. The jury rebellion was believed to be the first to occur in American history. Judge Ito worked feverishly for two days to salvage his jury—and the trial itself.

Jurors were under increasing pressure as the trial dragged on month after month while they endured living conditions and personal restrictions normally reserved for felons. These included 261 days of enforced separation from home, family, and friends 24—hours-a—day, severe censorship of all television viewing and reading material; close monitoring of all phone calls, and spot searches of personal belongings and written notes and computer files (many were confiscated by authorities). In fact, the jurors were left alone only when bathing, when using the toilets, or during tightly controlled once-a—week conjugal visits. A number of jurors were abruptly dismissed when they were suspected of preparing book manuscripts describing the ordeal.

Judge Ito once again avoided a mistrial by persuading the weary jurors to return to the jury box so testimony could once again resume. The second incident occurred as defense attorneys continued their relentless demolition efforts on the mountain of forensic evidence submitted by the Los Angeles Police Department's crime laboratory. Much of the grilling took place during the nine days Dennis Fung spent testifying before the court in March and April.

Fung's conduct during his investigation was brutally attacked in cross-examination by the defense. When he admitted that a junior assistant had gathered most of the critical blood samples at the crime scene, the defense attorneys and O. J. Simpson himself actually congratulated him when he stepped down from the witness stand (although he was a prosecution witness). Defense attorney Johnnie Cochran, Jr., was reported in the press as saying outside the courtroom, "We're having Fung, we're having Fung," and Robert Shapiro distributed fortune cookies to some journalists while commenting in laughter, "These are from Hang Fung Restaurant."

After the fortune cookie comment hit the front pages and prime time news programs, Shapiro publicly apologized to the court and to Asian Americans (some of whom were already planning a public protest at the courthouse). He said, "My heart has been heavy all weekend if even one person has been offended, and for that I sincerely apologize." While the defense team tried to worm itself out of its predicament, the prosecution hammered away at its "timeline" prosecution theory. Everything keyed upon the critical hour when the police believe the murder occurred. The prosecution tried to prove that none of O. J. Simpson's witnesses, including Brian "Kato" Kaelin, could provide him with a solid alibi for that time period, and they were preparing to introduce the first scientific evidence based on DNA analysis of the blood samples taken at the crime scene. The racial issue was once again poised to seize the headlines in the testimony for the so—called "trial of the century." The trial and justice itself seemed to be "hanging in the balance."

***

The first time I went to Los Angeles at the command of the Lord, I was relieved when God didn't require me to go into the courtroom itself. I was perfectly content to remain in the Criminal Courts Building and pray for anyone and everyone God pointed out or brought to me. When my "time" was up, I gratefully boarded a jet for Canada, hoping and assuming that I wouldn't have to leave my home and my daughter again. God had other plans for me.

Throughout the month of April, I began to feel the call again. I struggled with the Holy Spirit over this because I knew I wasn't being summoned to simply pray in the bowels of that courthouse this time. God told me a week before I made the second trip to Los Angeles that I was to pray a prayer for the court in person right in front of the judge, the jury, the attorneys, and all the trial participants. He said He was going to expose my prayer assignment to the 0. J. Simpson case for His own purposes.

The idea of offering a prayer in a courtroom out loud made me very nervous, but God told me He would be with me and His power would give me the strength to do it. I said, "Lord, I feel like I am going to go to the cross. But if it's Your will, then I'm going to do it." Once I made my decision (or should I say "my second decision"), I faced the "doing" of what I'd promised.

I didn't preplan the trips to Los Angeles because these trips weren't things I wanted to do. If you want to know how my trips happened, then it went something like this: I decided to obey God Thursday, and by Friday I was gone. If I decided on Friday, then by Monday I was in Los Angeles.

I wasn't "excited" about being at the O. J. Simpson trial—I didn't even know why the man was famous. In the beginning I knew nothing about Simpson, or about the crime he was accused of committing. But I *did know* that I didn't like leaving my home and daughter. Yet God again pressed a burden upon my heart to minister prayer to that court—and this time I knew He wanted me to pray openly, *publicly*, and *out loud* for the court! I could only reply, "Lord, I don't know how I'm going to do it. What are they going to do to me? Are they going to put me in jail? Only You know."

That Thursday in Toronto, I decided to trust God and take the risk, and by Friday I was in Los Angeles, meeting Rev. Smith at the airport. I will never forget the Monday morning that Rev. Smith and I arrived at the Criminal Courts Building in Los Angeles at 6:00 am. We arrived early to stand in line for a pass or ticket to the court gallery. Of the 80 seats available in the courtroom, only seven back-row gallery seats were available for the public after pre-assigned seating for selected journalists, family members, and various officials were designated.

Day after day, an average of 30 people would show up for the "lottery" drawing to get one of the seven tickets to the trial proceedings. That morning, 45 people were waiting for a ticket. If God had *really* sent me to pray for the court that morning, then He was facing His first opportunity to confirm His command with a miracle. I had never been in the courtroom up to that point, and I couldn't help but think, *I've picked a unique time for my first exposure to the court. I don't even know where to pray the prayer.* Any hidden or suppressed hope that I might not get a ticket didn't last long. My ticket was the third number called out from 45 other numbers that morning. When my number was called, I knew God had worked a miracle for me to get into the courtroom.

As I waited to board the elevator to the ninth floor, I was surrounded by lawyers, reporters, and other court observers. I had already said good-bye to Rev. Smith, who would remain on the first floor to support me in prayer while I was in the courtroom, and a reporter came over to me and asked, "Are you a lawyer?" I guess I looked like a lawyer, because out of habit I had taken care to present a professional appearance at the court. (I was very aware of the poor image many Christians portray in public settings through inattention to appearance, bearing, and manners.) Under the inspiration of the moment, I quickly said, "I'm a lawyer for Jesus." Surprised, he said, "What are you going to do here?" I smiled and said, "I'm going to pray."

The reporter was from the *Los Angeles Sentinel.* I didn't know it at the time, but the reporter pool was continually trying to find something new and novel to write about so they could satisfy the never-ending demands of their editors and readership. This reporter promptly told all the other reporters, "That lady over there is going to be praying in the courtroom-be ready for something unusual." I knew nothing about that, and as I sat in the back row of the gallery that morning on my very first public appearance at the O. J. Simpson trial, the entire gallery of journalists and broadcast news reporters was watching me and trying to figure out what I was going to do. They didn't realize it, but I was *already* praying quietly.

My first order of prayer concerned the extraordinary number of guards and bailiffs present in the courtroom that day. I started to pray silently, "Lord, why are there so many guards here today? Would You please put them outside so I can offer the prayer You have given me?" I was also concerned about the timing—the Lord didn't tell me what time I would be offering the prayer, so I was as uncertain as the media gallery was! I almost got up two times to say the prayer, but in each instance I sensed it was not the right time. My first prayer was answered that morning when most of the guards left the courtroom, but then I dropped into a deep sleep! In fact, when I finally opened my eyes, I saw all the guards trooping back into the room! I felt like I had missed God's divine opportunity to pray, and I began to get restless. I thought, "Oh Lord, I feel like a little loser," but the Holy Spirit said, "No, it is time to go out of the courtroom."

It was about 11:00 a.m., so I excused myself during a break in the proceedings and went out to have lunch with Rev. Smith. I found him reading downstairs, and then the same newspaper reporter walked out of the elevator. He had left the courtroom to find out if I was still going to pray. He joined us for lunch, and when we were settled, he asked, "Are you supposed to pray quietly during the trial or what?" I told him, "No, I'm going to pray loudly." I think that got him excited because he leaned forward and asked, "Can you give me the words? I want to put your prayer in the paper first." I said, "But I didn't do it yet! How can I give you the words before I pray them? I can't give the prayer to you-you'll just have to wait until I pray the prayer.

Then you will know." He shook his head and said, "I won't be here because I have another appointment." At that point I sensed he was just making excuses in the hopes I would give in and give him a "scoop." I thought, *that's just too bad. I can't do that.*

The reporter and I returned to the courtroom after lunch and Rev. Smith resumed his vigil on the first floor. I was still feeling a lingering disappointment because I felt I had somehow failed God, and I felt alone. I was wishing that Rev. Smith could have joined me in the court gallery. Then I began to hear angels singing, which really made me wonder if I was hearing things. All of a sudden I could see them surrounding me on the right and the left in the spirit realm. *Maybe this **is** the afternoon I will do the prayer!* I thought. I still didn't know what time the prayer would come, although I knew what the prayer was going to be.

Within moments, I felt the power of God pulse through my body. On May 1, 1995, at 1:02 pm, shortly after the jurors had filed in and taken their seats, I rose from my seat and went to the opening gate. I felt like somebody was lifting me up from the back. I didn't even know how I had arrived at the front of the gallery. Everything in the courtroom was in order and Judge Ito was about ready to reconvene the court. But everything just stopped when I fell to my knees, lifted my head to the heavenly Father, and said these words in a loud voice before the whole world, totally oblivious to the television camera and clicking shutters of the film cameras: "Father, Father, I am asking You in Jesus' name to open the heavens and give peace and strength to this court."

A hush fell over the courtroom and time seemed to stand still. No one moved until after the last word passed from hearing. Even judge Ito was surprised, although he had the best view of the courtroom from his elevated bench and with the help of his video and audio surveillance system the reporters privately called the "Ito-cam." Yet at the same time, he seemed to welcome the prayer in a court that had been encountering so much strife and confusion.

I saw O. J. Simpson turn around in surprise and then smile, as did Johnnie Cochran, Jr., Robert Shapiro, and the other defense attorneys, as well as Marcia Clark and the other assistant prosecutors. A strange peace seemed to fall over the room with that prayer, and I felt a sweet release in my spirit. I had done what God had called me to do. Only after the prayer was finished did sheriff's deputies come to escort me out of the courtroom.

God told me later that when that courtroom prayer was broadcast by satellite and described in newspaper accounts all over the world, He was answering the fervent prayers or countless believers from all over the world. Obedient Christian prayer warriors had petitioned Him in their churches and homes for a supernatural demonstration of His presence in that California courtroom, and He had given them a visible sign that He had assigned an intercessor to the case on their behalf and under His authority.

As a result of that prayer, and the many prayers of saints before that, the plans of Satan to trigger race riots in Los Angeles, New York City, and other major US. cities were thwarted, and Satan was unable to wreak havoc on God's Kingdom. I praise God for His intervention in answer to the prayers of the saints. He saved many lives from destruction and preserved many buildings from the ravages of arson and looting. In the midst of stressful and confusing times, God's Word offers the supreme comfort for believers. It declares that God is a good God, and Satan is a defeated foe. The Gospel of John declares, "The thief cometh not, but for to steal, and to kill, and to destroy: I am come that they might have life, and that they might have it more abundantly" (In. 10:10).

I didn't know that morning that God was going to arrange for the broadcast of that simple prayer to the whole world over television and radio via broadcast satellite. My first inkling of the magnitude of my task came when I sat in that courtroom and saw the TV camera and microphones. I said, "Lord, I don't want this thing to be broadcast in Toronto. I don't want anyone there to see me here." Oddly enough, I learned that for some reason, the live television report on the prayer didn't reach Toronto. It went nearly everywhere else in the world, but not to my hometown. I didn't want people in Toronto to see me and say, "Well, what is she doing there?" I didn't want people to know about my assignment because it was a secret thing I was doing for the Lord. I didn't want it exposed.

When I rose to my feet, the sheriff's deputies quietly followed me through the doors to the hallway and then they returned the way they had come. They already knew who I was; the deputies had been sitting near me during the whole prayer, and once they walked me out of the courtroom, I just left. My immediate task was finished, so I didn't have to remain in the courtroom any longer.

I remained in Los Angeles for four more days. I spent my time praying for the trial participants, interceding for the hurting families in the case, and covering the volatile race relations issue in constant prayer. Meanwhile, I told Rev. Smith that my daughter was on my mind, and I was looking forward to stepping out of the confusion and bright lights of the O. J. Simpson trial and into my slippers at home.

***

Before Tara Persaud returned to Los Angeles for the second time, I spent most of my time making preparations for her arrival, praying for her and our assignment, representing the

Lord among the media representatives on the twelfth floor of the Criminal Courts Building, and ministering among crowds of visitors, reporters, and sightseers on the sidewalks outside the building. One of our more interesting "partners" in the cause of Christ during those long months was a man named Larry Mays. He was dedicated to fulfilling one purpose—every time television cameramen or news photographers assembled by the courthouse entrance to film an incoming celebrity, attorney, or spokesman connected with the trial, Lany positioned his huge poster displaying John 3:16 squarely in view of the cameras directly behind the spokespersons. I considered us to be a "Holy Ghost tag team" of sorts.

God moved quickly to meet some of my housing needs and to provide quick availability to our assigned task. My first and perhaps most important contact was with my news photographer friend, George Redy. Not only did he open countless doors for us in the courthouse, but he also opened up his own home to me, as I noted earlier. An attic room in his house became my first "home away from home" during the 0. J. Simpson assignment. Whenever Tara returned to Canada, I stayed on in Los Angeles and continued to lay the groundwork for the next visit.

At one point I began to suffer from a serious infection in my leg that continued to get worse and worse. I ended up staying in the hospital for three days while doctors tried to figure out what was going on. I wound up leading the doctors through the sinner's prayer, and then my leg got better. Perhaps I landed in the hospital specifically for that task.

A major breakthrough came the day I tried to visit 0. J. Simpson in his cell at the Men's Central Jail, an annex to the Los Angeles County Jail complex downtown. Unlike the few celebrity visitors such as the Rev. Jesse Jackson and Rosie Grier who were able to see Simpson, I was unable to get through the screening process. (The defense attorneys as signed a staff member to the full-time job of screening the mountain of visitation requests to see their famous client.) However, God had sent me to the jail for a different kind of ordained appointment.

During my short visit to the Men's Central Jail, I met Pastor Murray, who pastors one of the largest churches in the LA area. He invited me to his church, and that is where I never also, and she graciously agreed to make the apartment available for me *at no charge!* This divine arrangement was to become a crucial blessing as the length and gravity of our joint treks to the Criminal Courts Building began to increase as the trial moved slowly toward a conclusion in the following months.

CHAPTER 6

We Pray the "Sinner's Prayer"

On May 10, 1995, the prosecution called Dr. Robin Cotton to the testimony stand and launched what it hoped would be its heaviest blow against 0. J. Simpson and his team of attorneys. Cotton, a biochemist and laboratory director at Cellmark Laboratories in Germantown, Maryland, dropped a bombshell when she stated that sophisticated DNA tests proved that a drop of blood found near the bodies of the victims matched 0. J. Simpson's DNA, and that blood found on a bloody sock at the foot of the defendant's bed matched the DNA of Nicole Brown Simpson.

Dr. Cotton was the first witness to link Simpson to the murders through her genetic tests. Despite fierce crossexamination by defense attorney and DNA expert Peter Neufeld, the researcher's contention seemed to be unshaken and very damaging to the defendant's case, in the opinion of most legal observers.

Week after week, the prosecution continued its efforts to translate complex DNA lingo and forensic procedures for taking blood samples into everyday language. The DNA testimony was followed by nine grueling days of testimony by the Los Angeles County Coroner, Dr. Lakshmanan Sathyavagiswaran, who defended his department's handling of the investigation, and graphically described how the victims died at the hands of a knife-wielding attacker. In the wake of incredibly detailed technical testimony; complex displays on "ELMO," the electronic graphics system used to zoom in on evidence photos and diagrams; and constant objections and daunting cross-examinations by the defense; the prosecution committed what many believe was the final error in the presentation of their case.

It has been said that on June 15th, the prosecution team had a working lunch together between sessions of the court Marcia Clark and her team of about ten attorneys from the Los Angeles District Attorney's office wanted to fine-tune their strategy as their presentation of witnesses and evidence wound down to a conclusion. They left the luncheon in agreement that they would not require or ask the defendant to try on the "bloody glove" found by Mark Fuhrman on the grounds of O. J. Simpson's estate. They felt the case was strong enough without the demonstration.

There was only one problem: Christopher Darden, the co-lead prosecutor in the case, was unable to attend the meeting—and he was slated to take the floor that afternoon. The message was passed along in a written note, but Darden evidently didn't get a chance to read it before the trial proceedings resumed that afternoon. He petitioned the court for permission to have 0. J. Simpson try on the glove in front of the jury. The demonstration backfired badly and many believe it fatally weakened the prosecution case when Simpson struggled before a TV camera to pull the glove onto his hand over sheer latex surgical gloves.

Over the next few days, the prosecution scrambled to prove the gloves shrank in size due to exposure to blood and other elements. Marcia Clark played a videotape that showed Simpson wearing the same type of gloves while doing a sports broadcast, and claimed they were the same pair; most observers said it was too late—the damage had already been done. On July 6th, the weary prosecution team, led by a visibly fatigued Marcia Clark, rested its case after presenting more than 92 days of testimony, 488 exhibits of evidence, and calling 58 witnesses to the stand. The defense team meanwhile prepared to call its first witness to the stand on the following Monday, July 10th.

***

I had been home less than a month when the Lord began to deal with me again about returning to Los Angeles on assignment to the O. J. Simpson murder trial. I felt that Rev. Smith and I were just beginning to get acquainted with Johnnie Cochran, Jr., and the members of his team, but we still weren't on a cordial basis. The first time we met I was allowed to pray for him and Mr. Shapiro personally. The second time they saw me, I was kneeling at the gate to the courtroom area, praying publicly before a TV camera and still photographers for peace in the courtroom. This time I was being sent to do something altogether different. Reluctantly, I notified Rev. Smith in Los Angeles, bought my airline tickets, and boarded a plane on Friday, June 16, 1995. The day before, unknown to me, 0. J. Simpson had struggled to pull on a bloody glove before wide-eyed jurors.

The court reconvened the following Monday morning and Rev. Smith and I met Johnnie Cochran, Jr., and the rest of the defense team by the freight elevator as usual. This time, we specially asked Cochran to have dinner with us so we could talk personally with him. He shook his head and said, "Do you know how many people are trying to get in touch with me?" We told him, "We are not those people, and we are not trying to get in touch with you. We are God's ministers, sent for you." He just stepped into the elevator with his team and kind of shooed us off.

We learned later that Johnnie Cochran, Jr., was a sad man at the end of that day. Despite his team's tremendous breakthrough the week before with the "shrunken glove" debacle, he suffered a setback that day when Judge Lance Ito bluntly turned down one of Cochran's more important motions or objections. We know the setback was serious because, the very next day, when we greeted him at the elevator as usual and when Rev. Smith told him I wanted to pray for him, he openly admitted to us, "I need prayer." While his entire defense team stood and waited, Cochran dropped his briefcase and received prayer. Things went altogether differently in the court that day, although the prosecution team was beginning its last week of testimony and preparing to rest its case. (One of the lawyers on O. J. Simpson's defense team was a Christian and the other lawyers often looked to him for spiritual help. He told me privately one time, "I can see you're anointing. Keep praying")

It was on this third trip that God began to speak to me about Johnnie Cochran, Jr. "*He needs to pray the sinner's prayer,*" He told me. He also said the same thing about Cochran's Jewish team member, Robert Shapiro. I couldn't believe that God wanted me to lead two of the most aggressive and verbally combative trial attorneys in the United States in public prayers of repentance and commitment to Christ. My faith was pushed to the limit on this one, but I made up my mind to obey God anyway. What was the worst that could happen? They could only say, "No." Now I had to wait for the right opportunity.

When Johnnie Cochran, Jr., walked down the hall toward the freight elevator the next morning, I asked him, "Would you like to pray this morning?" Without hesitation, he said, "Yes." Then I felt a supernatural boldness come over me as I asked him, "Would you like to go over the *sinner's prayer?*" He looked at me and said, "Yes."

I was so focused on my latest assignment that I can hardly remember how many people were in the hallway that day, but I know there were quite a few. As usual, there were two guards stationed on either side of the elevator door, along with some standby security personnel. Then there were a number of people in the defense team waiting while I prayed the words of the sinner's prayer, and while Johnnie Cochran, Jr., repeated the prayer after me with his head bowed. Evidently, a number of people present that day were amazed that this prominent black attorney would yield himself to my ministry like he did that day, but God was the one doing the work, not me. After he completed saying the sinner's prayer, Johnnie Cochran, Jr., asked me to pray for the court that day, and I did. As soon as he looked up and turned away to enter the elevator, Robert Shapiro walked up.

I asked Mr. Shapiro the same thing: "Would you like to pray today?" He said yes too, so I asked him the big question as well: "Mr. Shapiro, would you like to say the sinner's prayer?" Once again he said, "Yes," and bowed his head. Afterwards, the irony of the situation hit me full force. There I was, a woman from Guyana, South America, the mother of a daughter slain by a jealous, knife—wielding ex-boyfriend, praying the sinner's prayer with a respected Jewish trial lawyer from Hollywood, California, only moments before he would continue his defense of a black American sports hero accused of brutally slashing his ex-wife and her friend to death in a fit of rage.

If I ever doubted it before, I could not doubt it any longer: Miracles still happen. Robert Shapiro quietly prayed the sinner's prayer with me with his head bowed in full view of his peers and security personnel. Regardless of what these two men say about that June morning near the freight elevator, I know that I fulfilled my commission for that day when I publicly led them in the sinner's prayer confessing that Jesus Christ was Lord. How they conduct their lives after that prayer will forever be a matter between them and their Creator.

From that day on, I ministered to them whenever God asked me to, delivering whatever message He gave me for them. It was during this third trip that the Lord warned me in advance about catastrophic events and a physical crisis facing Johnnie Cochran, Jr. Both sides were still arguing over the "glove incident" and there was a lot of emotional "heat" in the courtroom that day. The situation was so tense that Judge Ito chose to push the proceedings right on through the lunchtime (something he rarely did) without a break. Rev. Smith and I were waiting and praying in the first floor lobby of the Criminal Courts Building when the Holy Spirit suddenly told me that the enemy (Satan) was extremely angry over some of the things being unveiled in the case that day, and he was about to strike out at Johnnie Cochran, Jr. I had the clear impression that Cochran would suffer a heart attack immediately after he stepped off the elevator unless God intervened! I also saw a vision or picture of two plane crashes and an undersea earthquake in my mind's eye.

I felt so weak at that moment that I could hardly stand or even hold my Bible in my hand. All I knew was that God was doing something in me. I told Rev. Smith about what I was seeing, and I told him that I thought the Lord wanted me to meet Cochran the moment he left the courtroom. (I assumed it would be for the lunch break.) Rev. Smith and I made our way to the private elevator and greeted our friends, the sheriff's deputies, again. We prayed, watched, and waited while the noon hour slipped by. Then 1 o'clock came and went. We knew something was going on because the court hadn't recessed for lunch. Finally at 2:30 that after noon, the defense team came down the freight elevator. I quickly stepped directly into the elevator with Cochran and moved behind him.

I felt I was supposed to place my hands over his head as if I were protecting him, so I did it and began to pray earnestly for his protection. I could hear noises in the hall as the press began to rush toward the attorneys, and I suddenly fell a sharp pain in my own heart—as if an attack meant for Johnnie Cochran, Jr., had been diverted to me instead. Then it passed and I walked the defense attorney all the way out to his car while the press corps followed closely behind us. Cochran knew what I was doing the whole time we were in the elevator, and he cooperated with me, almost as if he sensed the importance of my unusual actions.

Just before the defense attorney got into his car, I told him in a serious tone, "Mr. Cochran, don't answer any questions today. It's important." Despite the barrage of questions from correspondents and news reporters, the usually talkative Cochran refused to answer any questions that day, and he simply drove away, leaving me and a crowd of frustrated journalists there on the curb. (The reporters for the many TV and radio networks, newspapers, and magazines were some of our most consistent supporters and friends during the trial. I hated to encourage one of their most faithful sources not to talk, but on that particular day I felt Johnnie Cochran, Jr.'s life was in danger the longer he stayed in the courthouse area. I simply had to obey what God was telling me.)

The Holy Spirit had already warned me that the enemy intended to wipe out Johnnie Cochran, Jr. I know this sounds "spooky" and "super spiritual," but that is what I sensed. I strongly suspect that the Holy Spirit kept the court working until 2:30 pm. just to keep Cochran contained in one place for a period of time. (The enemy must have been furious. When we returned to our hotel room later that evening, we heard news reports confirming that *an earthquake* and *two plane crashes* occurred just off the coast near San Diego—at the same time of day I received the warning from the Lord in the hall of the courthouse!)

It was during that Visit to Los Angeles that Johnnie Cochran, Jr., called for me at the Ramada Inn. He wanted me to meet him at the courthouse to pray for his upcoming trip to Oklahoma City, Oklahoma. Evidently he had been retained to do some of the preliminary work to help defend an agricultural fertilizer company implicated in the trial of the men alleged to have bombed the Oklahoma City Federal Building using a homemade "fertilizer" bomb. Unfortunately, by the time I received the message it was too late to meet Mr. Cochran for prayer.

God also asked me to venture into the courtroom again for a special assignment one day at lunch when I'd gone to the washroom. When the Holy Spirit spoke to me about going into the courtroom, I said, "My God, how can I get into the courtroom? You know how crowded it is, and all the tickets have already been distributed."

When a friend and neighbor of Judge Ito died unexpectedly, the judge adjourned the court for a while that day so he could attend the funeral. That meant that seat allocations for the afternoon session would be distributed again by lot. Rev. Smith and I stood in line once again for a coveted ticket to the courtroom gallery, and both of us were hungry. The cafeteria smelled good, but we had to stay the course.

We received tickets for the "lottery" after two hours, and wouldn't you know it, my name was called first from among the 50 people hoping to be selected. Then the Lord told me what He wanted me to do. (I didn't know the specifics until that moment.) He wanted me to pray for Marcia Clark, the lead prosecuting attorney in the case. The prosecution team used a different elevator to reach the Superior Court from the basement of the Criminal Courts Building (the defense attorneys boarded their elevator from the main floor), so the only way to see Marcia Clark was to be in the courtroom gallery with her! God knows all things.

One man standing near me offered me $40 in cash for my ticket on the spot, and I said, "No way. You are not getting my ticket!" I wanted to know what God wanted me to do, and why. I am a curious person, and whenever God speaks to me about something, I habitually ask a lot of questions. Do you know what He wanted me to do? He began to tell me that Marcia Clark was desperately praying to God in secret. God told me that He really was hearing her prayers, but He couldn't do certain things she was asking because He had a very specific purpose for the case she was involved in. God loves us all, and He hears our prayers, but He does things based on His wisdom, His Word, and His plan, not according to our wisdom, circumstance, or desperation.

It was only expected that the enemy would plant a man right there beside me to offer money for that ticket. I told the man, "You can pay Rev. Smith for his ticket and take your chances [on being chosen in the 'lottery'], but I'm going up." I made it up to the courtroom and watched Marcia as she and her prosecution team worked feverishly to bring their case to a powerful ending before the defense took over. The stress levels she was enduring were incredible, and I knew the outward signs were only revealing a fraction of the deeper pressures aligned against her. My heart went out to her in that courtroom gallery, and I spent the entire afternoon interceding for her in the Spirit.

Although the Lord initially told me that third visit to Los Angeles would last 16 days, I felt at the end of that time period the Lord was telling me, "You are not leaving this hotel room until you *finish* this assignment. I want you to stay longer than 16 days." By that time, though, my mother's heart was nearly at the breaking point. I said, "Lord, I'm going back to my daughter—she is alone at home. If You want to do something to me, please wait until I am in Canada." (I said this because I felt that if I disobeyed God, then something could happen to me when He lifted His protection and favor off of me.) I didn't realize that God had a "cycle" going on in the trial. No one knew at the time what was about to happen with the "Fuhrman tapes" adjudge Ito's wife, a police captain with the Los Angeles Police Department. Had I known the case would come so close to a mistrial in the following weeks, I probably would have stayed on another week, but I was hurting and lonely for my daughter.

That was my third time away from home in a Los Angeles hotel room, leaving behind a decent house with plenty of open space. Every time I walked into a hotel room, I felt like saying, "My God, I can't stay here!" I faced a constant struggle between my own desire for privacy, peace, and my roomy home, and God's call to foreign cities and cramped hotel rooms. I felt terribly torn in my spirit over what to do. While I was taking a shower one day, the Lord said, "Daughter, I will not allow anything to happen to you. I have dispatched special angels to protect you." Then He showed me an angel, and I knew everything was all right. I told myself, "When I go home, He will talk to me about my assignments." I boarded a jetliner in Los Angeles on July 2nd, and as soon as I began to settle in at home, the Lord started dealing with me again about going back for another assignment.

***

"For as he thinketh in his heart, so is he" (Prov. 23:7a). The O. J. Simpson double-murder case uncovered the very worst aspects of American society. With each passing week, the hidden thoughts of countless Americans concerning race relations, male and female inequities, sexual and physical abuse, intimidation, and jealousy came to the surface in an unlovely tapestry of division, strife, and anger.

In the beginning, Tara Persaud often asked me questions about people and events that were common knowledge in America, but unknown to her. She said the Lord had brought up a name here, and a place there. Included among these names were Rodney King and Reginald Denny-a black man and a white man who were caught up in the swirling racial strife and violence of the crowded Los Angeles area. As I began to share with her the events associated with each of these men, I could see striking similarities between the forces at work in their crises, and the forces at work in the O. J. Simpson case.

The first recorded murder case on earth involved members of the same race and household, not some creature or beast from afar. Murder came from a "brother," a friend, even a fellow worshiper, and the root of the crime was jealousy. Abel was killed by his own brother right after "church service"!

Most prejudice stems from jealousy or self-righteousness, whether it is based on race, social or economic status, culture, or education. In Luke 10, Jesus spoke of a Jewish man who fell among thieves and was beaten up and left for dead. His fellow Jewish brother passed by, but did nothing to help. Neither did his Levite pastor. However, when a Samaritan came by (a stranger considered to be a second-class citizen because of his mixed blood), he picked up the wounded Jew, took him to an inn, and cared for him. This man's physical "salvation" came from a "stranger" instead of his so-called "brothers" in blood and faith. Was it any accident that even in Jesus' ministry, His own hometown did not receive His ministry, but the Samaritan "strangers" received it? Jealousy is a dangerous sin that breeds every kind of prejudice, rejection, hatred, and violence toward those we fear or envy.

> *And when He was come into His own country, He taught them in their synagogue, insomuch that they were astonished, and said, whence hath this man this wisdom, and these mighty works? Is not this the carpenter's son? is not His mother called Mary? and His brethren, James, and Joses, and Simon, and Judas? And His sisters, are they not*

all with us? Whence then hath this man all these things? And they were offended in Him. But Jesus said unto them, A prophet is not without honor, save in his own country, and in his own house. And He did not many mighty works there because of their unbelief (Matthew 13:54-58).

After decades of armed tension during the "Cold War," the collapse of the U.S.S.R. was caused not by the efforts or threat of NATO forces, but by serious problems within the Soviet Union itself—many of which were rooted in jealousy and bitterness over perceived inequities. So it is with our nation and even with the Church of Jesus Christ. Although the various nations and groups within the old Soviet Union could have pointed fingers of blame at the members of the NATO alliance, they knew all too well that the real problems producing the collapse of communism came from within their own ranks. All of us need to remember *that the people who do not look or live like us are not automatically our enemies!*

One of the most shocking facts about inner—city crime is that most of the crimes are actually "black on black" or "Latino on latino" crimes. This fact is lost in the roar of angry voices as whites accuse blacks of murdering whites, and blacks accuse whites of murdering blacks. Even a casual glance at the history books provides some revealing (and shocking) answers to these questions.

In 1994, a shocked world witnessed live television reports confirming mass tribal genocide in Rwanda. Both the killers and their victims shared the same skin color, but that did not make them brothers. When millions of people died during World War II on the European front, most of the "white" victims of war were killed by "white" soldiers in acts of war. These men "looked alike," but that did not make them brothers, did it?

White-skinned Germans killed six million white—skinned German Jews and millions of other white-skinned Slavic Europeans and Jews—all in the name of supposed "racial purity"! In recent years, the countless acts of aggression and murder during the massacres in the Nigerian civil war, the Angola civil war, the El Salvador civil war, the Bosnian civil war, and during the Lebanese "war of attrition" and the Iraqi intrusion into Kuwait, were all people of the same "stock" killing one another.

We must learn our lessons from the past so we can live in a future not ruled by the past.

Several years ago, race riots threw Los Angeles into a state of chaos in reaction to a videotape of Los Angeles police officers brutally beating an African-American motorist, Rodney King. Two things struck me about the case (things that were totally lost in the heat of blind race-centered prejudice): First, it was a white man—a man with a different skin color from Rodney King—who made the revealing video tape of the illegal beating and turned it over to television news personnel because he thought the beating was wrong. The second fact concerns a white truck driver named Reginald Denny who unknowingly drove his truck into a blocked intersection in the heart of the riot activity. When he was pulled from his truck and nearly beaten to death by black as— sailants while television news helicopters circled overhead, Denny the "white" victim was rescued by a "black" person at great personal risk.

The cure for what ails the nation is found in our Maker and in His unchanging Word, which declares, "And [God] hath made of *one blood all nations of men* for to dwell on all the face of the earth, and hath determined the times before appointed, and the bounds of their habitation" (Acts 17:26). So much for "pure bloodlines" and racial prejudice.

In the book *Animal Farm* by George Orwell, some pigs led a rebellion against the owner of the farm and overthrew him after accusing him of being a parasite and mistreating the animals. When the pigs took over leadership of the farm, they treated all the animals fairly in the beginning, even posting an inscription at the entrance of the farm that read: "All Animals Are Equal."

However, it didn't take long for the pigs to add the discriminatory phrase, "But some are more equal than others." When animal racism was introduced to the farm, the inferior animals began to suffer, even more than when they were under man's leadership. Orwell undoubtedly wrote this story to address more serious problems in human society. Racism is not a thing with which to tamper. It has a subtle tendency to take us deeper and deeper into darkness, eventually leading us into total spiritual blackness.

An old maxim says, "A good seed is known for the shoot." We know that pride goes before a fall, and the Lord admonished us all to humble ourselves, and *He* will lift us up. In the Lord, the best way to ascend to higher heights is to be humble. Only Jesus Christ has the power to set us free from our problems.

The things we must embrace, meditate upon, and work toward are those things that come from the very heart of God, and such things are given to us from His Holy Word, the Bible. We are not made for self-glorification, but for the glory of God. Diversion from the purpose for which we were made is sin. As Christians, we are supposed to focus on Jesus Christ, who is the author and finisher of our faith (see Heb. 12:2).

CHAPTER 7

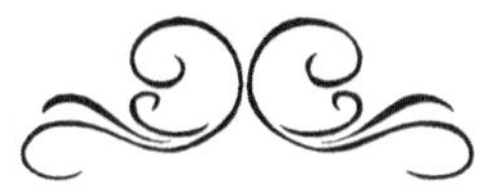

Secret Things Always Come to Light

July of 1995 was a landmark month for both sides in the O. J. Simpson double-murder trial. The prosecution rested its case after months of grueling effort to establish a solid case without benefit of a murder weapon, an eyewitness to the crime, or even a verified time of death for the victims. Despite the problems, the prosecution built a strong case based on mountains of circumstantial evidence and extremely technical DNA analysis of blood samples from the crime scene and from 0. J. Simpson's house and vehicle.

The defense called its first witnesses to the stand: Arnelle Simpson, the defendant's grown daughter; then his 73- year-old mother, Eunice; and lastly his sisters, Carmelita Simpson-Durio and Shirley Baker. Although their testimony describing a much kinder and gentler O. J. Simpson brought a welcome change of atmosphere to the courtroom, a grim battle had suddenly arisen outside that Southern California Superior Court chamber.

At some point after the prosecution rested its case, a phone tip was received by private investigator Patrick McKenna, who was working on the Simpson case from Johnnie Cochran, Jr.'s law offices on Wilshire Boulevard. The tip concerned tape recordings that might prove the prosecution's lead witness was extremely racist, thus potentially nullifying any and all testimony he had provided in the Simpson case.

McKenna reportedly told *The New York Times* that he called a college professor and would-be screenwriter living in Winston—Salem, North Carolina, named Laura Hart McKinney. McKinney had been working on a screenplay about the negative attitudes of big city police officers, particularly those directed toward female law enforcement officers. She was in a Los Angeles cafe when Detective Mark Fuhrman noticed her working on her laptop and asked her about her project. For the next nine years, McKinney con ducted taped interviews of Fuhrman as background for her screenplay entitled "Men Against Women."

McKenna quickly realized that those audiotapes contained explosive racial expletives and personal accusations aimed at key female officers high in the Los Angeles Police Department. They amounted to a lethal land mine with the potential of compromising much of what the prosecution had struggled to build over the previous months. The only problem was that McKinney did not want to get involved; there were indications that she was hoping to sell her story instead. Cochran's investigator was referred to the woman's Los Angeles attorney for further negotiations.

Matthew Schwartz, the LA. attorney representing Laura Hart McKinney, refused to supply the tapes or to allow his client to travel to Los Angeles to testify in the trial, so the "Dream Team" filed a legal motion in Forsyth County Supe rior Court in Winston-Salem, North Carolina.

While defense witnesses continued to testify before the court in Los Angeles, outside the courtroom the defense team began to shift its entire case in a new direction, gambling that somehow the newly discovered "Fuhrman tapes" would make their way into Judge Lance Ito's courtroom. Nothing came easy. The North Carolina judge ruled on July 28th that McKinney did not have to testify or turn over her audiotapes because she was working on a "fiction" work, and the content of the tapes would therefore have no value in the California case.

Cochran and Shapiro immediately had their team of legal experts file an appeal to the North Carolina State Court of Appeals, where the lower court finding was overturned. The lower court was required to issue a summons to Laura Han McKinney to testify in Los Angeles, and to release all of her tapes, transcripts, and related documents to the defense team upon request. When the prosecution team in Los Angeles heard the shocking news, they immediately filed a subpoena to get copies of all the tapes and documents.

By September 5th, the so-called "Fuhrman tapes" had made their way into the courtroom for "admissibility" hearings while the jury was held in sequestration, unaware of the new turn of events. Everything the defense team had worked for since the summer of 1994 had seemingly been dropped into their laps. All summer long and into heated court arguments in January, 1995, the defense attorneys had tried to portray Detective Mark Fuhrman as a racist who was capable of planting evidence to frame their African-American client. Each time their efforts fell short due to lack of firm evidence that Detective Fuhrman had not changed his ways in the past ten years. The "Fuhrman tapes" could potentially transform the defense claim into an established fact, and both sides in the case knew it.

From the moment the first tape was played (and broadcast internationally), the image of Los Angeles Police Detective

Mark Fuhrman was transformed from that of a top-notch, straight-talking career detective with a believable face into an aggressive hate-filled racist with a compulsively foul mouth. As one Associated Press report stated, "the jury was absent but the world was listening in." Everything prosecutor Christopher Darden had expressed as a fear in court arguments in january now became a very real threat to the prosecution team. Race was no longer simply a side issue to the criminal charges against O. J. Simpson; it had become the central issue that could determine the validity of the entire mountain of evidence presented by the prosecution. The prejudice of Mark Fuhrman was quickly becoming a filter through which everything else in the case would be viewed. The prosecution was worried about the tapes' impact on the jurors when they were revealed for the first time in the courtroom.

Many commentators, stunned by the derogatory contents of the tapes, publicly voiced their concern that another "Rodney King riot situation" was in the making, recalling the violent days following the Rodney King beating, and the subsequent publicity revealing blatant police brutality. From that time on, observers on the street and in the courtroom noticed a new tension and emotional abrasiveness descend on the proceedings. Police stepped up their security measures, and the crowds outside the courtroom began to clash more and more each week as the trial continued its slow advance to a tortuous close.

***

From the day I returned to Canada from my third trip to Los Angeles on July 2nd, God was speaking to me about new dangers facing the O. J. Simpson trial. I began to feel an unusually heavy burden to pray for the trial, as if countless lives were hanging in the balance. As usual, I was hoping that I wouldn't have to leave my home again for another trip to Los Angeles, and I was growing increasingly concerned about my daughter, who was staying with friends and still trying to recover from her sister's death. The added weight of loneliness she faced when I had to leave for extended periods only seemed to make things worse for her. Yet that was the time the Lord told me to quit my job. I have to admit that I just didn't agree with this request. (And I kept on "disagreeing" with it while God relentlessly pursued me requiring obedience.)

I called Rev. Smith in California and told him about the Lord's direction to quit my job. I also told him I just couldn't do it. "Reverend Smith, I'm not quitting my job! I'm making good money, and I get paid holidays. I also earn additional income from my part-time work as a real estate agent. Besides, no one is helping me pay for this prayer assignment in Los Angeles. You know about the bills, Reverend Smith. You know I pay for them all myself. Every plane ticket, every hotel bill, and every meal is paid for out of my pocket. What am I going to do when I can't keep filling that pocket?"

Despite my protests and explanations, Rev. Smith sided with God. He urged me to trust God and simply obey Him. Finally he caught a plane to Toronto and prayed with me in person about the situation. After we talked and talked about it, and after much prayer, God put a desire in me not to go back to work. One hundred percent of my income was coming from my job with the Canadian government and from my real estate work, but I also knew my ministry work with the O. J. Simpson case was important too (even though it wasn't something I was doing for financial gain). All I could hope for was that someday God would reward me for the sacrifices He was asking me to make.

Rev. Smith flew back to Los Angeles and I quit my job. Once that step was taken, God began to speak to me once again about going back to Los Angeles—this time for four weeks! I knew I was in for a really intense time of warfare on this trip, but we were about to discover and experience a whole new level of "intensity" this time around.

I reluctantly packed, bought my airline tickets, and prepared to board the plane for Los Angeles once again. It was even harder to leave Roxanne. I sensed that she was at an important point in her life, and it was hard to turn her over to God so I could take this trip. In the end, the urgency of the Situation in California pressed on me whether I was in prayer, in my car, or working in my kitchen. The call to go had become too insistent to ignore and put off any longer. I said goodbye to my daughter and boarded the plane while fighting back tears, hoping I would never have to leave Toronto again.

I arrived at the Los Angeles International Airport on Monday afternoon, July 24th, only 22 days after leaving there for Canada at the end of my third trip. As usual, Rev. Smith was faithfully waiting for me at the gate, and had prepared everything for me in advance. I told him about the urgency I sensed for this visit, and we made arrangements to go directly to the courthouse every single day to pray and intercede.

The most alarming thing I began to sense was that the direction of the trial was turning a corner. It would soon veer away from attempts to puncture the "timeline" theory of the prosecution, which was an attempt to prove that O. J. Simpson had no alibi and had plenty of time to commit the murders. Instead I felt the defense would turn the case toward racial issues somehow. I felt this was both dangerous and necessary, but didn't know why. The pressure was extremely heavy during the last days of July and into August. Only later did I learn why.

As we went to the courthouse to pray day after day, my suspicions were confirmed about major changes taking place. On August 15th, three days before I was scheduled to leave

Los Angeles, Deputy District Attorney Marcia Clark boldly demanded thatJudge Lance Ito remove himself from the trial on the basis of a charge that rocked the watching world. For the first time, the existence of the so called "Fuhrman tapes" came to light.

Those audiotapes had been recorded over a nine-year period ending just the year before. Evidently the tapes included two highly explosive elements that the defense Wanted to bring forward:

1. The recorded voice of Detective Mark Fuhrman uttering racial slurs (specifically, "the n-word") 42 times, obviously contradicting his testimony under oath earlier in the Simpson trial that he had not spoken a racial epithet for a decade; and,

2. Fuhrman's disparaging remarks about the female officer who was his watch commander on the Los Angeles Police Department in 1985, Captain Margaret "Peggy" York (*who was also the wife of Superior Court judge Lance Ito*).

Marcia Clark demanded that judge Ito step down from the case to avoid accusations of bias and conflict of interest against the prosecution's lead witness. The judge openly agonized over the mean-spirited references to his wife. Millions of TV viewers watched as the judge fought back tears and read a statement that said, "I love my wife dearly, and am wounded by criticism of her as any spouse would be." The blight of racism and bigotry had even reached beyond the courtroom and a decade of time to bring pain to the family of the judge overseeing the case. The worst had just begun. The inflammatory statements on the "Fuhrman tapes" were about to ignite new flames of racism across the United States.

The O. J. Simpson case had hit the first crisis point I had sensed while still in Canada, and the trial came perilously close to being declared a mistrial that day. That was when I understood why God had called me to that Los Angeles courthouse to pray as I had never prayed before. The crisis came on August 15th when Marcia Clark demanded that Judge Ito disqualify himself from the case and defense coun- seljohnnie Cochran, Jr., urged the judge to remain on the bench to avoid a mistrial. Meanwhile, the disclosure of the tapes also triggered a full-fledged investigation of Mark Fuhrrnan by the Los Angeles Police Department's Internal Affairs Division, personally directed by the deeply embarrassed Police Chief, Willie Williams.

After consideration of the claims and heated arguments from both sides in the case, judge Ito narrowly avoided a mistrial by ruling that he would remain at the bench and rule on the admissibility of those portions of the "Fuhrman tapes" related to racial epithets and allegations that the police had planted evidence, while another judge would rule on the admissibility of taped references concerning Ito's wife, and her viability as a trial witness. From that point on, the 0. J. Simpson case took a permanent turn toward the "race question."

Prosecutor Marcia Clark backed down from her demand thatjudge Ito step down from the case, but just as I boarded a plane to return to Toronto once again, the battle began to determine how many, and which excerpts of Fuhrman's racial slurs would be admitted to court's evidence before the predominately black and female jury. The world knew the tapes existed, but now it would discover that the reality of their contents was worse than the rumor.

The very day I returned to Toronto, another Superior Court judge named john Reid ruled that judge Ito's wife, Captain Margaret "Peggy" York, had nothing relevant to add to the trial, so once again mistrial was avoided. If Captain York had been compelled to testify, then judge Ito would probably have been forced to disqualify himself from all or part of the case to avoid charges of conflict of interest. His withdrawal would have been basically the same as declaring a mistrial.

When I got home, I was still under a tremendous burden to pray for the case. Lives were still in the balance for some reason unknown to me, so I prayed. With the discovery of the "Fuhrman tapes," johnnie Cochran, Jr., and Robert Shapiro dramatically altered their case and began to charge that Mark Fuhrrnan and other white racist Los Angeles p0 lice officers had planted evidence to frame their client be cause he was a famous black man and a former football great who had been married to a white woman. From that point on tension levels in the courtroom and in cities and urban neighborhoods across the United States seemed to rise dramatically, with many people "taking sides" along race lines. Rev. Smith began to tell me about the changes he saw and sensed in the crowds of people gathered outside the Criminal Courts Building. Something was terribly wrong.

On Tuesday, August 29th, 11 days after I returned to Canada, 61 excerpts of different "Fuhrman tapes" were broadcast around the world from judge Ito's courtroom during a hearing to determine which excerpts would be admitted as court's evidence and played before the jury (which was still being shielded from news reports about the tapes). On Friday the Slst, Judge Ito ruled that only 2 of the 42 "expletive" excerpts on the tapes would be admitted as evidence, and Johnnie Cochran, Jr., angrily protested the judge's ruling, saying it was "cruel and unfair."

***

As I talked and prayed with Tara Persaud, it became more and more evident that God was about to uncover a terrible darkness that was invading some of the most important institutions of this nation.

Several years ago in Nigeria, there was a young man in his twenties who gave his life to Jesus Christ, but had somehow remained lukewarm. He loved the things of the world, and never did quite commit fully to the Lord. One day he became very ill and died.

The man's body was subsequently prepared for burial by a mortician and placed in a coffin. The coffin was taken to the grave site for burial, but before the grave diggers could lower the casket into the grave, the men were startled by a loud commotion. Someone was screaming and banging from inside the coffin! The shocked workers could clearly hear the words, "Take me back, Lord! Take me back, Lord! Take me back, Lord!"

They hurriedly backed away from the grave and lowered the coffin to the ground. Overcoming their fear, they managed to open the coffin and to their surprise discovered that the young man had come back to life! When the young man was helped out of the coffin, he was asked what had happened. He told the crowd of people that had quickly gath ered that when he died, be sensed that his soul was ascending toward Heaven when suddenly a big hand came from nowhere and grabbed him at a point between Heaven and earth. His eyes were opened, and he actually saw what Heaven looked like. "The glory of Heaven is indescribable," he told the amazed crowd. "I just wanted to be there right then."

That same invisible hand suspended him long enough to see the earth that he had loved so much before his death. It was so full of thick darkness that he felt he could have cut the dark cloak of misery with a knife. However, he also noticed that there were a few bright lights here and there. (When I heard him tell this story, I secretly hoped that I was one of the lights he saw!)

When I asked him about the words he was screaming at the grave site, he told me that when he screamed, "Take me back,

Lord," he was begging God to take him back to Heaven! He did not want to go back down into the thick darkness he saw covering the earth.

What this man saw is truly scriptural. The world is cloaked in darkness, and it is ruled by satan, whom the Bible calls "the prince of darkness." The apostle Paul painted a clear picture of our situation when he wrote to all believers, "For we wrestle not against flesh and blood, but against principalities, against powers, against the rulers of the darkness of this world, against spiritual wickedness in high places" (Eph. 6:12).

From a spiritual standpoint in Christ, the unsaved inhabitants of the world dwell in darkness. It is only when they are washed and transformed through the atoning blood of Jesus Christ that an inner light penetrates the darkness to make them a new creature, a bright light shining on a hill before all.

With the "mysterious" discovery of the Fuhrman tapes, the Lord was going to "Open a wound" to let it drain so our nation could move on to genuine cleansing and eventual healing of our racial hatreds, prejudices, and biases. In contrast to the patterns of mankind, who as a whole like to hide their weaknesses and disguise their sins, God knows that true healing will come when the hidden things are brought out into the light where they can be confessed, removed, and replaced with good things that bring life and peace. We still have a long way to go.

CHAPTER 8

The Trial Within the Trial

Late in the O. J. Simpson trial process—after the prosecution had already closed its arguments, in fact—the defense team totally altered its fundamental arguments after it unearthed and introduced the explosive "Fuhrman tapes." From that point on, Simpson's "Dream Team" shifted from its early plan to discredit the prosecution's "timeline" case to a secondary position, and instead launched on all-out attempt to portray white Detective Mark Fuhrman as a blatantly racist cop who planted evidence to wrongfully put their African-American client behind bars on false murder charges.

The new evidence seemed to prove the defense claims that Mark Fuhrman was still a racist despite his claims to the contrary while under oath. The "Fuhrman tapes" and new photographic evidence was used in a fast-paced effort to disassemble and discredit the prosecution's case and prove that Mark Fuhrman planted evidence and that other police personnel covered it up.

This new evidence that further established the obvious racial bias of Mark Fuhrman, seriously undermined the credibility of the most important evidence against O. J. Simpson- and enflamed the emotions of onlookers around the world.

Suddenly, the credibility of the prosecution's chief witness, a senior law enforcement officer in perhaps the most volatile homicide case in the history of one of the world's largest cities was all but destroyed. Months of detailed testimony and layered prosecution argument was instantly clouded in doubt. The defense regeared their arguments and in essence became "the prosecution against Mark F uhrman," knowing that if he fell, the prosecution's case would fall as well. Cynics and "informed commentators" around the world pointed to the O. J. Simpson case with renewed energy and confi. dently predicted the collapse of the American judicial sys tem and a return to the racial conflict of the 1960's.

The believability or credibility of witnesses is the central crux of every criminal case tried before a jury of "peers." The attorneys for the defense do everything in their power to discredit or lessen the believability of the prosecution's witnesses, and the prosecution lawyers do the same with defense witnesses. This adversarial process has caused many witnesses in criminal trials to say afterward that they felt like *they* were on trial in the courtroom instead of the accused. There is an assumption that mature American citizens impaneled on a jury will have what it takes to see past the courtroom antics of trial attorneys and to penetrate the defenses and tangled lies of untruthful witnesses. *The O. J. Simpson murder trial stretched this concept to the breaking point.*

The fairness of the US. judicial system rests on four im portant factors:

1. The individual sets of character values, prejudices, and biases individual jurors bring into the courtroom with them.

2. The morals, professional ethics, and methodologies of the attorneys presenting their cases before the jury,

3. The integrity and performance of law enforcement officers commissioned to fairly enforce the laws of the people without partiality or prejudice.

4, The ability of impartial judges to firmly guide all the parties in the court through the "fact-finding" and deliberation process in strict accordance with the law and established legal precedent.

When any one of these four foundations of the legal system are askew, the whole system is in danger of collapse.

***

When I returned to Toronto after my fourth trip to Los Angeles, my most urgent thoughts were focused on my daughter, Roxanne. Despite everything else that was going on, I had never forgotten her. I knew from that point on, I would have to take her with me for any out-of-town trips. She was at a place in her life where she needed to be with me.

More than at any other time, the Simpson murder trial seemed to fuel the fire of cynics and critics worldwide in late August and early September of 1995. That is when racism came to the forefront in everything. I *had* no idea what I was about to run into, but I did sense an unusual urgency when I prayed about the trial and the nation south of the Canadian border. Once again, I began to sense the familiar nudge in my heart—it was time to pack my bags again.

I called Rev. Smith and told him that Roxanne and I would be flying to Los Angeles. I felt that I had to be in California by Monday, even though that fell on September 4th— the

American Labor Day holiday. I didn't know the significance of the timing, but I knew it was important to the Holy Spirit, so I bought tickets for Roxanne and I and we boarded the plane early Monday morning.

On Friday morning, before my daughter and I arrived in Los Angeles, God had spoken to me about arriving in Los Angeles by the beginning of the following week. I had no idea that the day before, Thursday, Judge Lance Ito issued his decision to allow the jury to hear only two excerpts containing the racial expletive called "the n-word" which appeared 42 times among the 61 different segments of the "Fuhrman tapes." The court adjourned for the long Labor Day weekend early, and everyone concerned evidently hoped the importance of that ruling would be forgotten by the time they returned to "Department 103." It wasn't.

When judge Lance Ito reconvened his court on the Tuesday following Labor Day, the media was ready. That was September 5th, the day the jury listened to the two ap proved recordings from the infamous "Fuhrman tapes" for the first time. I was in the courtroom that day and watched the predominately African-American jury react to the venomous racial epithets spoken by Mark Fuhrman on the scratchy tape recordings. Some of them even seemed to flinch. Again and again throughout that day and in the days to follow, those statements were aired on television and radio news reports around the world. It wasn't a proud day for Los Angeles, or for the United States.

Earlier in the trial, Fuhrman's attorneys claimed that the detective's use of the "n-word," along with slurs againstjews, Mexicans, and female police officers, and statements about alleged tampering of evidence, beating of suspects, and other misconduct by LAPD officers, were only given as "police color," spoken in the persona of a fictional character. They said Fuhrman was trying to impress Laura Hart McKinney, the college professor and screenwriter who re corded Fuhrman's racist comments. McKinney was one of three witnesses that day who confirmed the LAPD detectives frequent and recent use of racial slurs—even when the tape recorder was turned off. The epithets on the tapes were shocking. They almost totally negated the value of Mark Fuhrman's testimony, who only 174 days earlier had testified under cross-examination before the same panel that he hadn't said "the n-word" even once in the previous ten years.

I listened as a witness named Kathleen Bell told the jury that she heard Fuhrrnan say out loud at a Marine recruiting station that all the blacks (he used "the n-word") should be "gathered together and burned." Natalie Singer also testified before the jury, which included nine African-Americans, that Fuhrman had told her, "The only good n-—is a dead n—--."

After defense attorney Gerald Uelmen successfully argued outside of the jury's presence that the evidence was absolutely critical to the defense case, the defense was permitted to call police photographer Rolf Rokahr to the witness stand. Rokahr told the jury he took pictures of Fuhrman pointing at evidence just before the sun came up on June 13, 1994 (the morning after the murder of Nicole Brown Simpson and Ronald Goldman)—*before* the detective went to Simpson's estate, not after he returned. The defense claimed this was different from Fuhrman's version of the story, and suggested that it proves the detective took the evidence to Simpson's estate to plant it there.

That same day, defense attorneys Johnnie Cochran, Jr., and F. Lee Bailey verbally sparred with prosecutor Christopher Darden over the number of witnesses brought forward to testify about Detective Fuhrman's use of racial slurs. Darden said, "This is not the trial of the people versus Fuhrman, not yet," but Johnnie Cochran, Jr., countered with the argument that race was an issue that could not be avoided. Allin all, the defense team brought three key witnesses to the stand to testify about Fuhrman's racist actions. Cochran even managed to persuade Judge Ito to allow the testimony the following day of a black man harassed and cursed by Fuhrman.

On Wednesday, September 6th, a fourth defense witness, an African-American communications repair technician from Chicago named Roderic Hodge, told jurors that Fuhrman arrested him in 1987 and leveled a racial slur at him as he was placed in a police cruiser. That same day, Mark Fuhrman appeared on the witness stand again in the absence of the jury. The first question defense attorneys leveled toward him was, "Detective Fuhrman, was the testimony you gave at the preliminary hearing in this case completely truthful?" Fuhrman immediately answered, "I wish to assert my Fifth Amendment privilege" (the part of the Bill of Rights that guarantees protection against self-incrimination).

Fuhrman issued an apology through his attorney while the trial was still going on. After the trial, the retired detec. tive admitted he was wrong and again apologized for his racist remarks on a national television interview in late 1996, but the damage had already been done in late August and early September of 1995. One of the television reporters for Channel 4 in Los Angeles said the Fuhrman tapes "rained out of heaven." Whether they did or not, God was apparently using those tapes to expose a serious racial problem that still smoldered below the surface of American society.

Although Mark Fuhrrnan's attitudes and personal prejudices actually had nothing to do with O. J. Simpson's guilt or innocence (either he committed the crime or he did not), he was a senior LAPD detective with a stated hatred and disdain for African-Americans and interracial relationships between blacks and whites. He was the detective who personally collected much of the most damaging evidence used against a prominent black sports figure accused of murdering his white ex—wife and her white friend. No one, not even the prosecution, was denying that Detective Fuhrrnan's racial biases had dramatically weakened the prosecution's case. For most of the day on September 5th, Marcia Clark and the rest of her prosecution team could do little more than sit uncomfortably through the extremely damaging testimony against Fuhrman, rising only occasionally to lightly cross-examine the witnesses.

O. J. Simpson's name was on the court docket as the accused, but the American nation was on trial as well, including her institutions, her beliefs, and the attitudes and actions of her citizens. The issues and heat in the trial seemed to bring to the surface the very worst aspects of contemporary American society, almost like the heat of a forge causes every impurity to rise to the top of molten metals in a crucible.

While the world watched, the debacle in Los Angeles seemed to demonstrate that American trial law often has everything to do with the equation of persuasion and almost nothing to do with justice. Each "side" won temporary battles through domineering arguments, personal attacks, and slick persuasive techniques, only to see their work washed away the following day or week by a new assault of arng ments from the other side. The O. J. Simpson case *may* be recorded in history as the landmark felony case of the century. It will *certainly* stand out as the ultimate display of the weaknesses inherent in the American jurisprudence system, and as an unmistakable symptom of the nation's eroding values.

As the trial continued to wind slowly toward a close, tensions remained high inside and outside the courtroom. Every expression and movement of the weary jurors were scanned and analyzed for hints about their moods and reactions to the case. From September 5th to the 15th, I continued to pray personally with Johnnie Cochran, Jr., other attorneys on his team, and from a distance, for the attorneys from the district attorney's office. I also felt a burden for the jurors whose worn faces clearly revealed the tremendous stress they were feeling.

I took Roxanne along with me to the Criminal Courts Building many times during that two-week period, introducing her to scores of media representatives, reporters, and photographers. Rev. Smith and I took her to the media "war room," and even took her along to our familiar spot on the first floor by the freight elevators where I introduced her to Johnnie Cochran, Jr., Robert Shapiro, and the rest of the defense team when they came in the morning for the trial. At last, my only living daughter was able to see for herself what I was doing all those times I left her in Toronto to fulfill my "assignment" in Los Angeles. She saw firsthand how I prayed for the key individuals on both sides of the courtroom, and why those prayers were so vital to the purposes of God in the O. J. Simpson case. just having her with me took a tre mendous weight off my shoulders. With both of us "on the case" together, my mother's heart could fully concentrate on the urgent issues of prayer I faced each day we were in Los Angeles.

Rev. Smith and I also took her along for our usual visit to O. J. Simpson's Brentwood estate on Rockingham Avenue where I passed along a message to O. J. Simpson through the guards at the security gate and through his family members who often came out to see us. Many of them had met us and prayed with us at the courthouse during previous visits. Roxanne's perspective was forever changed by her first visit to my "job" in Los Angeles.

Things seemed to go "the defense's way" the first week of September, beginning with the playing of the Fuhrman tapes in court, followed and supported by the testimony of four witnesses portraying Mark Fuhrman as a racist cop. On Thursday, September 7th, the defense team pressed judge Ito for permission to call Mark Fuhrman back to the witness stand as its final "witness" so they could openly accuse him of perjury *in front of the jury*, but he refused the defense bid very early in proceedings that day.

The disappointed defense team then urged the judge to tell the jury that Fuhrman had invoked his Fifth Amendment privilege, but again he refused their request. judge Ito told them the jury would only be told that F uhrman was "unavailable " for a court appearance. That made both sides unhappy. The defense team wanted the jury to know about Fuhrman's action, hoping they would perceive it as an admission of guilt, regardless of its true legal implications. The prosecution felt that since the detective had taken the Fifth Amendment outside the jury's presence, then it should re main there completely. Marcia Clark strongly objected to judge Ito's proposed compromise, claiming that even a statement from the bench about Fuhrman's unavailability would lead the jury to speculate about the detective's absence in a prejudicial manner Judge Ito responded by giving the prosecutors time to file an appeal of the ruling in a higher court.

The jury spent the next day in sequestration again as lawyers argued before an appeals court about judge Ito's proposed instruction to the jury about Mark Fuhrman's "unavailability." When all the arguments had been heard, the court rejected Ito's proposed jury instruction. The defense team filed its own appeal asking the appeals court to overrule judge Ito's ruling barring them from calling Detective Fuhrman to the witness stand again.

In another dramatic development on Thursday, just when it was assumed the defense would rest its case, the defense team announced that O. J. Simpson would not testify in court in his own defense. This infuriated Marcia Clark, who had waited for months for the chance to cross—examine the accused. Gudge Ito instructed the jury at the beginning of the trial that O. J. Simpson was not obligated to testify in court, since in American criminal cases, the burden of proof is on the prosecution.)

Defense attorney F. Lee Bailey explained to the press that "with the [prosecution] case in shambles, this just wasn't necessary. I didn't see What was left to be gained, when you have the chief witness, a law enforcement officer, refusing to testify because he might incriminate himself." Bailey said that Simpson's attorneys advised him not to testify after Mark Fuhrman appeared in court and invoked his Fifth Amendment protections against self-incrimination. The defense team felt that the devastating effects of Fuhrman's tape-recorded comments about racism and wrongdoing among members of the Los Angeles Police Department would be all that was needed to create "reasonable doubt" in the minds of the jury.

Although members of the prosecution team claimed that Simpson was trying to evade the witness stand, Robert Shapiro told *The Associated Press*, "OJ. has always wanted to testify in this case. He realizes like all of us that this jury is weary and his testimony would. prolong the case two to three weeks, and he's more anxious than any of us to get a verdict in this case."

More and more national polls and surveys were indicating that American opinions on the guilt or innocence of OJ. Simpson were beginning to fall almost universally along race lines. The majority of white Americans believed the former Heisman Trophy winner and National Football League starturned-actor was guilty of the murders, yet most non-white, and particularly African-American citizens, were strongly convinced O. J. Simpson was the innocent victim of a racist frame-up by Detective Mark Fuhrman and other corrupt white officers within the Los Angeles Police Department.

The tape-recorded statements Mark Fuhrman made to screenwriter Laura Hart McKinney alleging police brutality, discrimination against women on the police force, and racist actions in the field against innocent citizens captured the attention of US. Attorney General Janet Reno and the US.

Justice Department. Federal officials launched an official inquiry to determine if Fuhrman and other LAPD officers had manufactured evidence, targeted African-Americans for arrest, or infringed on the Constitutional rights of citizens as his taped comments suggested. An in-depth investigation was also launched by embarrassed officials of the Los Ange les Police Department and the Mayor's office as well. The dirty laundry was flying in the wind, and it was attracting far too much attention for the comfort of many elected officials around the country.

On Monday, September 11th, the "Dream Team" refused to rest its case until it had received a final decision from the appeals court about its request to recall Mark Fuhrman to the stand. Judge Ito, determined to keep the trial moving toward a conclusion, ordered the prosecution to begin its rebuttal. It was during these arguments that FBI footwear expert William Bodziak was called to the stand for the first time. His testimony jolted the "two-killer theory" that the defense team had carefully constructed prior to the discovery of the Fuhrman tapes.

Earlier in the trial, the defense team had brought in one of the most respected criminologists in the country to conduct an independent examination of the evidence at the crime scene. Dr. Henry Lee claimed he saw a fresh bloody shoe imprint at the crime scene, and presented photographs he had taken of several other imprints at the murder scene, along with evidence of what he said was a shoe print on an envelope that Ronald Goldman had used to return a pair of glasses to Nicole Brown Simpson.

Bodziak told the jury that the bloody imprint Dr. Lee claimed he saw actually never existed. He said the wavy line identified by Lee as a fresh imprint was actually an impression left by concrete tools when the sidewalk was poured for the walkway. The photographs of "other imprints" weren't even present in police photographs taken immediately after the discovery of the murders, and the bloody prints on the envelope were too small and irregular to be shoe prints. Legal analysts said Bodziak's testimony was dramatic and powerful enough to undermine the testimony of the defense witness. The testimony struck a powerful blow against the defense team's "two-killer theory" and seemed to breathe a fresh breath of life into the battered prosecution case that had just suffered through a week of proceedings on the explosive F uhrman tapes.

On Wednesday, September 13th, the court was in session behind closed doors on the ninth floor, and the streets outside the Criminal Courts Building were a study in tension. A large group of angry African-American men, including a number of Black Muslims in bow ties, had suddenly staged a march on the Criminal Courts Building, causing the sheriff's department to hurriedly evacuate the main floor and lock the doors. The sheriff's deputies were clearly preparing for the worst. While all of this was going on, I was sitting alone in the cafeteria praying for the court—unaware of what was happening on. the street outside the building. To this day, Istill can't explain how the sheriff's deputies somehow missed me when they made their rounds to clear out the first floor of the building. Rev. Smith had already left to attend a prescheduled prayer meeting elsewhere in the city and Roxanne was still at the hotel.

While I was still in the cafeteria, the Lord told me that militant Black Muslims were holding hands and advancing on the building. He told me the authorities had to lock up all the doors to the building because of the threat of potential violence. I thought, *Oh, that's great! They're expecting violence and here I am sitting alone in the courthouse cafeteria-caught right in the middle.* Then the Lord told me, "Go out into the front lobby and speak the word that I will give you."

When I left the cafeteria and stepped into the lobby area on the main floor, I saw three things that instantly con firmed the warnings I had received from the Holy Spirit. First, I saw armed sheriff's deputies swarming around the main floor with such urgency that they totally ignored me. Second, I noticed that all the doors were locked. I couldn't have left if I wanted too. Third, when I looked through the large plate glass doors leading out to the street in front of the Criminal Courts Building, I saw a large number of visibly angry black men moving toward the building. Prominent among them were Black Muslims dressed in how ties in the manner of the followers of the Rev. Louis Farrakhan. It was clear from their facial expressions, angry motions, and the kinds of things some of the men were carrying that at least some of the protesters intended to break down the doors of the building or break the glass!

Things had been especially tense in Los Angeles after the Fuhrman tapes surfaced, and emotions ran even hotter after most of the Fuhrman tapes were suppressed and when Mark Fuhrman invoked his Fifth Amendment rights in the O. J. Simpson case. Growing numbers of people, particularly in the African-American community in the greater Los Angeles area, were getting frustrated over the growing evidence of racial discrimination surfacing in the trial. They wanted the truth brought out and felt the shocking evidence in the Fuhrman tapes was being wrongly suppressed in the Simpson case. The potential for violence and bloodshed was evident, and everyone sensed that if violence did break out at the courthouse, then it would certainly spread throughout the entire Los Angeles area and even to neighboring metro areas within hours. Something had to be done quickly to avoid a deadly confrontation.

All I knew was that the Lord had spoken to my heart about certain words I was to say, and though I knew it would make me look pretty foolish, I was getting used to receiving unusual commands from God. I looked through the lobby doors at the advancing group of men crossing the street, pointed my finger toward them, and said out loud, "In Jesus' name, I command all of you to go across the street—now!"

There were sheriff s deputies in the lobby and in adjoining hallways, and though they didn't bother me or speak to me, they knew I was there. I've often wondered what they thought about that crazy scene of a little woman pointing her finger from inside the courthouse building toward a crowd of frustrated and angry men. I can almost see their eyebrows go up when they heard my words drift down the hallways telling the crowd outside to "go across the street." I don't know what the sheriff's deputies thought about my actions that day, but I do know that the group of angry and frustrated men approaching the main doors of the Criminal Courts Building that day *suddenly and inexplicably turned around and crossed the street!* I have faith in God, but I have to confess that I was really relieved to see those men turn around peaceably and return to the other side of the street. I think everyone in that building breathed a sigh of relief in that moment (and perhaps many of the men outside the building as well).

I looked through the windows for signs of any local police officers, sheriff's department personnel, or FBI agents, but everyone was in the building or out of sight. The action of the crowd was so unusual that I wanted to make sure there wasn't some police captain or FBI agent talking to the crowd with a bullhorn commanding them to go away. There wasn't. There was only one logical (or illogical) explanation for the sudden retreat of those angry Black Muslim protesters—God had showed up.

The Lord fully intended to pull back every concealing veil and reveal the racism and inequities rooted deeply in some of America's most revered institutions. He would not allow any violence or unwanted "help" from others to mar and muddle His message. I knew that God does not hate Mark Fuhrman or the Black Muslims, nor does He hate Hindus, atheists, or racially biased Christians, but He will always hate sin and anything in opposition to the gospel of His dear Son. It seems He has a special dislike for any doctrine of race hatred or racial strife that intertwines itself with human lives. The true gospel is the good news of Jesus Christ and His work on the cross to redeem *all mankind*, not just one or two privileged or supposedly "superior" races. Racism simply has no place in the agenda or the family of God.

Wednesday the 13th was also the same day that Johnnie Cochran, Jr., announced in court that he wanted to summon FBI Agent Frederic Whitehurst to the witness stand to testify about problems in the crime lab. His announcement was a hint of What would take place in the courtroom the following week.

On Thursday, tensions rose another notch when the ap peals court rejected the defense team's request that Mark Fuhrman be required to appear in court again and be compelled to "take the Fifth Amendment" a second time in front of the jury. Judge Ito followed the instructions of the appeals court and barred the defense team from recalling Mark Fuhrman to the stand. As the trial ground closer to an end, I could sense a growing fear rising up in the city and even in the courthouse. There was a clinging sense of impending disaster or doom that refused to be ignored. What would happen if O. J. Simpson was found guilty? Would interracial violence erupt across Los Angeles? Would the terrible riots the nation witnessed in the Rodney King beating case sweep across the city once more? Many believed that if violence erupted again, it would be much worse and more widespread than ever before, perhaps rivaling the nationwide strife seen at the peak of the civil rights struggles of the 1960's—only without the non-violent influence of the late Dr. Martin Luther King, Jr.

Federal, state, and local law enforcement agencies, particularly in large metropolitan areas, quietly began to prepare for the worst, and I sensed that Christians around the world felt a supernatural call to prayer at the same time. An unholy violence had birthed this sad legal process, but I felt God was not going to allow violence to be the chief fruit of this trial. He was out to reveal hidden sin and corruption for the sake of correction and healing. I never doubted the importance of my intercession assignment to this landmark case, but the urgency of my mission became even clearer with each day of the trial in September.

On Monday the 18th, Roxanne and I boarded a flight for Toronto, Canada, while on the ninth floor of the Criminal Courts Building, the prosecution conditionally rested its rebuttal. Somehow I knew it was merely a temporary calm before the storm.

CHAPTER 9

Prelude to a Verdict

The final weeks of September 1995 were marked by dramatic eleventh-hour turns and surprises in the OJ. Simpson case that surprised and dismayed observers and participants on both sides of the case. One day, the court proceedings were going on upstairs as usual when sheriffs deputies found a suspicious package outside the building. The trial continued undisturbed while sheriff's deputies cleared spectators away from the front of the Criminal Courts Building until the package was inspected. Explosives specialists confirmed at the site that the package did not contain a bomb and the circus in the street reassembled.

On Tuesday, September 19th, one day after Roxanne and I left Los Angeles for Toronto, the defense team launched a last-minute two-pronged attack on Federal, state, and regional law enforcement agencies involved in the OJ. Simpson case, hoping to have much of the evidence gathered and presented in the case thrown out. Its first goal was to prove that LAPD officers wrongfully entered and searched OJ. Simpson's estate, thus making all evidence gathered there inadmissible. Then the defense team alleged that corruption within the ranks of the LAPD and flawed evidence-gathering, handling techniques, and analysis procedures there and even in the FBI crime lab had tainted key evidence in the case.

The first wave of this assault was directed toward Detective Philip Vannatter, the 25-year LAPD veteran who was the senior officer of the detective team including Tom Lange, Mark Fuhrman, and Mark Phillips, that made the initial visit to OJ. Simpson's house just after 5 o'clock in the morning after the murders.

Early testimony indicated that at 5:50 am, Detective Vannatter made the decision to enter the Simpson residence after no one answered the buzzer at the security gate, and after Fuhrman told the other officers of his discovery of a haphazardly parked white Ford Bronco outside the Simpson estate with bloodstains on the door handle. It was Mark Fuhrman who actually climbed over the security wall and opened the gate to the Simpson estate without a search was rant. It was also Fuhrman who discovered the infamous "bloody glove" on a service walkway behind "Kato" Kaelin's room in the Simpson compound.

The defense brought forward an FBI agent and two brothers who were reputed Mafia associates protected as government informants under the Federal Witness Protection Program since 1984, to testify about comments Detective Vannatter made about his visit to the Simpson estate. Government informant Larry Fiato claimed that Detective Vannatter told him injanuary that he went to 0. J. Simpson's house because "the husband is always the suspect." The statements were allegedly made by Detective Vannatter in a hotel room during a meeting with the Fiato brothers, a deputy DA, and Vannatter's partner. Fiato also said Vannatter made a similar statement during a smoke break a month later at the courthouse during a mob prosecution case.

FBI agent Michael Wacks was also present at the courthouse that day, and he said he overheard Vannatter's comments.

The defense claimed that Vannatter already considered Simpson a suspect *before* the detectlves made a warrantless search of Simpson's estate, which would make all evidence gathered there inadmissible in court. But Craig Anthony "Tony the Animal" Fiato proved uncooperative on the witness stand, and he finally stated that he had dressed up his story about Vannatter's statements just to "shake up" the FBI agent assigned to him. "I was pimping him. . .I was exaggerating the circumstances to aggravate him. . .I got one over on him." Evidently "Tony the Animal" was rumored to have been romantically involved with Denise Brown, the sister of the murder victim, Nicole Brown Simpson, and enough of this came through in the dialogue between defense counsel and the witness to anger the Brown family and prompt the family attorney to demand an apology from the defense team for making such "disgusting and outrageous" insinuations.

The testimonies of Larry Fiato and FBI agent Wacks were considerably weakened when they admitted under cross-examination by the prosecution that they felt Detective Vannatter was "kidding around" at the time. Agent Wacks said that during the conversation, he believed that Vannatter's statement was just a "sarcastic jibe" at the defense team's efforts to paint their client as a Victim of some police conspiracy.

If the defense claim had been upheld, much of the evidence gathered at the SimpSon estate that day, including the "bloody glove" and most of the DNA evidence apparently linking blood samples at the murdersite with those from the Simpson estate, could have been thrown out. They charged that since Simpson was not an official suspect at the time the officers entered his estate without a search warrant, the evidence was illegally obtained (a violation of the Fourth Amendment to the Constitution, which protects citizens from unreasonable searches and seizures). The defense challenged the police entry very early in the trial, claiming the police had acted "in bad faith" by implying on their written request for a search warrant that Simpson had fled the state (when they had already reached him at his hotel in Chicago and been promised he would return on the next available flight), but the argument was disallowed.

The chief contributions of the Fiato brothers were some drama and lighter moments of humor with their bizarre clothing and flamboyant "mobster roles" in the courtroom. They were by far the court's most colorful witnesses, and they agreed to testify on the condition thatjudge Ito impose a total television and audio blackout to conceal their identities. (Ironically, only a few hours after Judge Ito imposed the media blackout of the Fiato brothers' testimony, Craig Anthony "Tony the Animal" F iato appeared in a pretaped interview on ABC TV's popular "Good Morning America" morning program with his face in full View! Evidently the Fiato brothers weren't as concerned about exposing their identities as they ledjudge Ito to believe.)

Los Angeles Police Commander Keith Bushey testified for the prosecution that he personally ordered a detective at the crime scene to go to the Simpson estate that morning to notify Simpson of the murder of his ex-wife, hoping he could notify the Brown family before the media reached them. In the end, the court felt that Bushey's testimony and other evidence established the legality of the police entry into the Simpson estate without a search warrant. Vannatter testified that O. J. Simpson was not a suspect on the morning they went to his estate, but as soon as it was clear there was pertinent evidence at the estate, he called for a criminologist and a legal search warrant and declared the estate an official crime scene.

Johnnie Cochran, Jr., had announced a week before the Fiato brothers appeared to testify, that he wanted to summon

FBI chemist Frederic William Whitehurst to testify before the jury that Roger Martz, an FBI toxicologist, had given slanted information about test results on blood samples gathered at the murder scene and at Simpson's estate.

The defense team also hoped to recall Martz to answer their allegations. His scientific analysis and testimony about complex tests on blood samples was especially damaging to the OJ. Simpson defense.

Whitehurst, formerly the FBI's leading explosives residue analyst, had previously criticized the operation of the FBI crime lab during the prosecution of suspects in the 1993 World Trade Center bombing. The Bureau modified its claims about the chemical composition of the bomb after Whitehurst spoke up about his concerns. The FBI and Federal prosecutors managed to convict the suspects anyway, but Whitehurst claimed he was demoted to the job of "analyzing paint" for forensic evidence because he "rocked the boat."Judge Ito denied Cochran's request in a written ruling on Wednesday the 20th, noting that the jury was already weary, and that the defense had already called a witness to challenge Martz' testimony. That also meant that Roger Martz would not be recalled to the witness stand either, effectively cutting off the defense team's second plan of attack on the prosecution's case.

***

The two defeats encountered by the defense team on Wednesday were just the beginning of a series of disappointments the "Dream Team" would experience that week. Some of the longest and most difficult days of the trial still lay ahead for everyone connected with it, and though I was thousands of miles away in Toronto, Ontario, I could sense an incredible burden of prayer beginning to build in my heart and in the Body of Christ.

I occasionally glanced at news reports to see what was going on in the trial, and when I felt prompted by the Holy Spirit, I would pray for a specific aspect or problem in the case that day. Each time I was surprised at the effects of prayer when offered in obedience to the Spirit's direction.

I realize that since most of my personal contact was with members of the defense team, readers may begin to feel that I was a "prayer advocate" for O. J. Simpson and his attorneys. For that reason, I have to emphasize again that I was as Signed to pray for the O. J. Simpson *trial*—for every aspect and "side" of the trial, not merely for one party. By all logical and psychological arguments, I should have had every reason to despise O. J. Simpson. After all, didn't my own daughter die at a young age at the hands of a jealous, knifewielding man in an attack hauntingly similar in many respects to the deadly attack that took the lives of Nicole Brown Simpson and Ronald Goldman?

I strongly sensed that God intended to work through the O. J. Simpson case to uncover hidden evil at the core of American society and institutions. I also had a deep compassion for the *victims* of the trial. I'm not only talking about the two young victims who were viciously murdered—I am also talking about the *living victims*, the family members and friends of the victims who have to carry to their graves the pain, the heartache, and the permanent sense of loss created by that tragedy. I am a firm believer in the consolation, restoration, and healing power of God, but I also know how painful it is to lose someone you love to violence. God preserved and healed my wounded heart, but I will always feel a sense of loss when I remember my beloved Shelley, and "what might have been."

When I watched any of the televised court proceedings after I returned home to Toronto on September 18th, my heart was often turned away from the details of the case itself to the wounded faces of the three families, the living victims of the crime. Some of them I'd met and personally prayed with many times, but I could only pray from a distance for others. But each family became more and more special to me as the case moved closer to a conclusion. I sensed that although their hearts were hardened by the painful events of the trial, their hearts were nearly broken by a growing sense of hopeless loss. I could hear their hearts' cry, "Will our lives ever be 'normal' again? How can we go on like this?"

Although I had been praying for all three families from the beginning—the Simpsons, the Browns, and the Goldmans— I began to sense a growing urgency to pray for the members of the Brown and Goldman families in particular. There seemed to be a particular despair and brokenness in their faces that, in turn, broke my heart. The grieving Simpson family hoped to see O. J. Simpson freed from jail and reunited with his children. The Brown family had lost a dearly loved daughter, but they took some solace in the innocent children she left behind as a legacy of her beauty and personality. The Goldman family, however, would never regain what they longed for the most—no matter which way the trial went. Ronald Goldman was gone forever, and no court proceeding or earthly action would ever bring him back. He had never married or presented a grandchild to his parents before his untimely death at the age of 25.

Meanwhile, the Spirit of God would often warn me about specific developments or areas of need in the case, and in those times I shut down my schedule to concentrate on prayer until I sensed the specific crisis had passed. Otherwise, I learned about the court case in my phone conversations with Rev. Smith, who remained in Los Angeles and regularly stationed himself at the courthouse, or the same way everyone else did during the last two weeks of September—through the media. (My daughter tended to keep a much closer watch on daily trial developments than I did.) There were several days when I felt a fresh urgency in my spirit to pray over the unfolding events in the courtroom. I knew emotions were running higher than ever, and both sides of the case were really feeling the effects of the yearlong court battle. Yet despite their fatigue, the things the key participants said and did in the trial could literally affect the future of their nation.

***

Judge Lance Ito rocked the defense attorneys on Thursday morning, September 21st, with his announcement that the jury panel would not be restricted to considering only a first-degree murder charge. The announcement was made during a hearing held away from the jury's presence to tie up matters concerning final instructions to the jury. It was perhaps the defense team's most devastating defeat in the trial. They had planned from the beginning to ask O. J. Simpson's jurors for an "all or nothing" verdict on the charges of first-degree murder, but now the panel would also be allowed to consider a lesser charge of second-degree murder.

Defense attorney Gerald Uelmen argued that the instruction would "undercut the defense" and said the jury should only have to choose between one of two verdicts: either "guilty of first-degree murder" or "innocent" in the slashing deaths of Nicole Brown Simpson and Ronald Goldman. The defense had argued all along that premeditation was a necessary element of the crimes. Until the judge's announcement, two crucial elements were required for the jury to find O. J. Simpson guilty of first-degree murder: premeditation and deliberation. The defense hoped to persuade the jury that the crimes *were* premeditated and deliberated, but that their client was not capable or guilty of premeditating, planning, and committing such a crime. All the defense had to do was to establish "reasonable doubt" about the first-degree charges, but Uelmen warned that the unexpected option of a second-degree murder charge "invited the jury to compromise."

The defense knew the jury could now find O. J. Simpson guilty of the lesser charge of committing murder in a moment of rage and passion (without the restrictions of premeditation or deliberation), and the new development caught the defense totally off guard. They were especially concerned about a "compromise verdict" by jurors who might feel sympathy for O. J. Simpson but at the same time want to convict him of a crime of passion.

Prosecution attorneys argued in the hearing that Goldman was an unintended victim who was in the wrong place at the wrong time, and that Ms. Simpson possibly was murdered in a moment of rage and passionjudge Ito replied, "I don't think there's any reasonable interpretation that would not indicate that Mr. Goldman's presence at the crime scene was by sheer chance."

Brian Kelberg, a prosecution attorney, said outside of court, "A jury may find that the evidence is not sufficient beyond a reasonable doubt to convince them the defendant weighed the pros and cons of his actions," but Simpson could have killed "in a moment of sheer anger and rage. They have to look at what role rage and anger played." With those brief statements, the prosecutor had revealed the prosecution's closing strategy for the final arguments and summations of the O. J. Simpson double-murder case.

Judge Ito reviewed lists of "special instructions" each side wanted to present to the jury in final arguments, and again the "Dream Team" heard the judge reject almost all of their 38 special instructions in the hearing. Most damaging Was Ito's refusal to allow an instruction that would focus on Mark Fuhrman's key role in the investigation, and would allow them to throw out all of his testimony if they felt he testified falsely about anything.

Instead, the judge said he would tell them they could distrust the testimony of any witness who was "willfully false" while believing other parts of his or her testimony that they felt was probably true based on the evidence.

Judge Ito also rejected a defense proposal to tell the jury to determine whether or not there was contamination of key evidence about blood, hair, or fiber samples *before* they considered its relevance to the case. Even more upsetting to defense attorney Barry Scheck, who is a nationally recognized expert on the use and interpretation of DNA evidence in court cases, was the judge's rejection of a proposed instruction about statistical probabilities of DNA "matches." Scheck wanted them to be told that a high statistical probability of a DNA "match" doesn't necessarily determine the likelihood that the defendant committed a crime, but the judge wanted the jury to draw its own conclusions from the evidence.

The defense attorney was visibly upset because he argued that most of the blood evidence used by the prosecution for its case was actually "planted" at the crime scene to frame Simpson, and even if that could be proven to be untrue, the blood samples were contaminated and therefore unreliable as evidence. He didn't want the jury to accept the DNA evidence from the samples at face value without considering defense arguments that would throw out the evidence altogether.

Another major defense setback came with the news that the California Supreme Court had denied the defense appeal that jurors be given more details about Mark Fuhrman's conspicuous absence from the witness stand, even though they had heard tape recordings of him saying "the n-word" in total contradiction to previous testimony under oath. That meant the jury would not know that the detective had invoked the Fifth Amendment protection to avoid nating himself when asked if he had lied to the court.

Friday, September 22nd, brought another surprise that caught the prosecution off guard and outraged the families of the murder victims.

With attorneys on both sides of the case poised to rest their cases in preparation for closing arguments the following week, Judge Ito asked O. J. Simpson to state for the record his decision not to testify in his own defense. When the judge said earlier that he intended to have Simpson make the statement in court, Prosecutor Marcia Clark expressed alarm. She felt the public statement was part of a defense plan to influence public opinion through the media, a plan that might even reach the jurors through family members following the trial. "This is an attempt to get testimony be— fore the jury without cross—examination," Clark said. Please don't do this, your honor. I beg you." But Ito agreed with defense attorney Johnnie Cochran, Jr., who said, "He has a right to speak to the waiver. They can't stop him."

O. J. Simpson stood up to make his statement immaculately dressed in a brown suit with matching shirt and tie, closely watched by the judge, a crowd of attorneys, the audience in the courtroom, and the ever-watching media. Then he calmly delivered a bombshell to the court while the world watched on live television:

"Good morning, your honor. As much as I would like to address some of the misrepresentations about myself, and my Nicole, and our life together, I am mindful of the mood and the stamina of this jury.

"I have confidence, a lot more it seems than Miss Clark has, of their integrity and that they will find out as the record stands now, that I did not, could not and would not have committed this crime.

"I have four kids. Two kids I haven't seen in a year. They ask me every week, 'Dad, how much longer?' I want this trial over."

Then Judge Ito interrupted Simpson's unauthorized statement to pointedly ask, "You do understand your right to testify as a witness and you choose to rest your case at this time?" and Simpson nodded. The judge said, "All right. Thank you very much, sir," and nodded for the defendant to sit down. It was the most Simpson had said in public since June 17, 1994, before his arrest on murder charges.

Just before Judge Ito's interruption, two radically differ. ent reactions in the gallery were heard by those nearby, Sounds of quiet sobbing came from Simpson's grown daughter, Arnelle, seated on the front row; while on the other side of the room and the arguments, the grieving father of Ronald Goldman, Fred Goldman, bitterly muttered, "Murderer. Murderer."

Marcia Clark was livid. After Judge Ito thanked Simpson for his reply, she immediately demanded that Simpson take the stand so she could question him, but Ito didn't respond to her angry protest. Johnnie Cochran, Jr., then made the routine motion that the court acquit his client of all charges, but Judge Ito quickly denied the motion and summoned the jury for the last time that week—only four days short of a full year after the jury selection process had begun.

When the jury was seated, Johnnie Cochran, Jr., rose and addressed the jury and Judge Ito: "I'm very pleased to say that we have no further testimony to present at this time, and as difficult as it is, the defense does rest at this time." Then Marcia Clark, who had become the clear leader of the prosecution team, stood to tell the jury, "We ask the court to receive all of the people's exhibits, and the people rest."

With those words, all opportunity to introduce new evidence, ideas, or witnesses was over. The jury of nine African-Americans, two whites, and one Hispanic, had heard from a parade of 126 witnesses since January 31st, when the first witness took the oath before the jury. The prosecution had called 72 witnesses for arguments and rebuttal, and the de fense team had called 53 witnesses (for their primary arguments and one rebuttal witness.

Judge Ito instructed the jury in the key points of the law for the next 45 minutes, and told them they would return to the jury box to hear final arguments on Tuesday, September 26th (the exact one-year anniversary of the day jury selection began, and after nearly 37 weeks of continuous sequestration). The mood of the jury became abundantly clear when Ito asked them if they would be willing to work nights during the next week to conclude the arguments and begin deliberations. They responded with big smiles and enthusiastic nods and one juror said, "Yes!" That prompted the increasingly somberjudge Ito to remark with a smile, "We have one unanimous decision already."

Then the defense listened intently as the judge began to explain to the jury that even if they acquitted O. J Simpson of first-degree murder, they could still find him guilty of second-degree murder. He also instructed them on the precise meanings of key legal terms such as reasonable doubt, premeditation, and express malice. He waded into the sticky area of witness credibility by telling the jurors, "You are the sole judges of the believability of a witness." Then he told them they should consider a witness's demeanor, bias, motive, and character in "assessing truthfulness." He carefully avoided any mention of Mark Fuhrman in keeping with prior rulings by higher courts.

Judge Ito was carefully eyed by attorneys on both sides as he gave the jury instructions for properly considering DNA evidence, evaluating expert testimony, and weighing the effect any laboratory errors might have on scientific evidence.

As soon as the court was adjoumed, the waiting media were met in the lobby by the late Ronald Goldman's father, and he was fuming over O. J. Simpson's unorthodox statement of innocence in the courtroom. Fred Goldman told reporters, "If he [Simpson] had a statement to make he should have gotten on the d— stand and said something, and not been a coward and been unable to have the prosecution question him." (Goldman was referring to the fact that had Simpson chosen to testify in his own defense, then Marcia Clark and the other prosecution attorneys would have been able to cross-examine the defendant while he was under oath.)

With his voice quavering in anger and his arm around his wife, Goldman commented on O. J. Simpson's statements about not seeing two of his children for a year, "I will never see my son again. How dare he throw that up?" Goldman also told reporters, "It's disgusting what he did. It's disgusting that his 'Dream Team'—'Scheme Team' maybe is more accurate-would come here and stand in front of you and tell you it was his right to make a statement in court. And it's disgusting tome also that the judge tolerated it."

The courthouse finally cleared out and the TV crews stowed their equipment after the last evening broadcast. Everything seemed to be on hold until court would resume the following Tuesday in what would be the final round of the O. J. trial. It was during this critical week of summations that God began to speak to me about returning to Los Angeles. I didn't know the details yet, but I began to suspect that the week of September 26th through the 29th would lead to something unexpected and momentous. I knew this because, for some reason, God was specifically telling me I was to be in Los Angeles on Monday, October 2nd.

CHAPTER 10

Marked for Death

Monday, September 25th, was Rosh Hashanah, the jewish New Year. At the request of the Goldman family and counsel on both sides, Judge Ito called a court recess for the day. It was unlikely either side rested well Monday evening, however. Final summations were to begin Tuesday with the prosecution leading off.

Both sides were faced with the nearly impossible task of helping the jury make sense out of nine months' worth of testimony and argument that had generated 50,000 pages of transcripts and accumulated a total of 857 pieces of evidence! Each side hoped to somehow swing 12 individuals around to their particular point of view. To make matters worse, those 12 individuals had been separated from their families for nearly a year—and they were followed everywhere they went; their television viewing and reading material were closely censored, and they had to ask permission to do something as simple as place a phone call to their mother. They were in no mood to be persuaded about anything—except getting back home as soon as possible.

On Tuesday morning, lead prosecutor Marcia Clark began to deliver what may have been the toughest closing argument she had ever tackled. The plan was for her to handle the first half of the closing arguments, and for Deputy District Attorney Christopher Darden to handle the second half. Clark would again appear before the jury later that Week to deliver the prosecution's final rebuttal after final closing statements by the defense. Clark's rebuttal statements would be the last arguments the jury heard just before its members received final instructions from Judge Ito prior to beginning deliberations.

Clark faced a sullen and worn—out jury that morning. In previous weeks, their attention had been drawn more to the racist remarks of Detective Mark Fuhrman than to the mountains of evidence her team had presented to link O. J. Simpson to the violent murder of Nicole Brown Simpson and Ronald Goldman. She had to win them over in an "eleventh hour" effort without the benefit of eyewitnesses, a murder weapon, or bloody clothing that would conclusively link O. J. Simpson to the crime. Time was working against her. She stood up to speak to the jury members that Tuesday morning on the 461st day after the slashed bodies of Nicole Brown Simpson and Ronald Goldman were first discovered.

The success of Christopher Darden's arguments the following day would depend to a great extent upon the success of Marcia Clark's presentation that morning. Due to the devastating impact of the Fuhrman tapes (which were officially introduced as evidence in the case only a number of weeks before), the prosecution now faced a crisis. Clark was caught in a situation with more than a year's worth of argument and persuasion and approximately $9 million worth of taxpayer investment in the balance.

The prosecutor spent most of the day Tuesday convincing and reminding the members of the jury that they were seated in the OJ. Simpson murder trial, not the "Mark Fuhrman prejudice trial." She tried to shift their eyes away from Fuhrman to the mountains of evidence the prosecution had presented about the murder and the accused. Although Fuhrman had been exposed as having racist views, she tried to prove that his personal biases didn't affect the evidence that pointed to O. J. Simpson as being a killer. Hundreds of people had contributed to the fact-finding effort in the case, not one.

Clark had barely begun to discuss the key evidence presented in the murder case when her presentation was suddenly interrupted by the ever-present media. While she was talking about the testimony of witnesses and medical personnel who saw or examined cuts on O. J. Simpson's hands the day after the murders, the lone camera operator who operated the only courtroom television camera using two remote controls, tried to zoom in for a close-up of Simpson's right hand. Simpson was seated at the defendant's table as usual, but he happened to be writing a note to one of his attorneys at the time. That note was, of course, privileged information between an officer of the court and a client.

Judge Lance Ito, his bench outfitted with laptop computers and a joystick-operated security video system he used to monitor information being fed to national media outlets and the world, noticed the slip in media protocol. He instantly flipped one of four switches on his control unit and cut the video and audio feeds to the networks and the outside world. He was forced to interrupt Marcia Clark to reprimand the operator. The judge imposed a media blackout that remained until he met with media representatives and was satisfied that proper guidelines would be followed. He allowed the media group to resume broadcasting an hour later after levying a stiff $1500 fine on CG Productions. CG Productions was the pool broadcast media group providing audio and video feeds to the media networks and representatives on the twelfth floor and in "Camp OJ.," the broadcast media compound across the street from the Criminal Courts Building.

Marcia Clark then resumed her closing statements and repeated key points in the prosecution arguments that pointed to O. J. Simpson as the murderer. She noted the defendant's lack of an alibi about his whereabouts when the murders occurred, along with the possible motives he had for committing such a crime. Clark wanted to demonstrate that there were powerful motives and established behavior patterns that, when linked to all the evidence, pointed to O. J. Simpson as the murderer. She said, during her closing arguments, "I think that was the last straw for him. He was abandoned by Nicole, he was abandoned by Paula [Barbieri, his girlfriend at the time], and that's why we're here." Clark knew that every argument she presented well on Tuesday could become a stepping stone on Wednesday for prosecutor Christopher Darden (and every failed argument could become a pothole endangering everything that followed).

On Wednesday morning, Christopher Darden continued the final arguments for the prosecution. While Marcia Clark dealt with the vast body of forensic evidence presented by her team, Darden's job was to focus on the history of violence that haunted the 17-year relationship of OJ. Simpson and Nicole Brown Simpson. Somehow the prosecution hoped to take the jury beyond the public image of O. J. Simpson the movie star, sports commentator, advertising pitchman, and beloved football star. Darden told the jury, "We came here today in search of justice. You will have to be the judge. . .as to whether any of us found it today." Then he began to rehearse the sad litany of a marriage gone bad and a relationship sprinkled with jealousy and frequent incidents of spousal abuse. His goal was to prove that O. J. could and did commit violent acts against Nicole Brown Simpson when motivated by jealousy and hurt.

First Darden set the stage for murder by describing the disturbing events on the day of the murder that could have driven the defendant over the edge of self-control to commit a deadly act. "A call to Nicole Brown Simpson the day of the murders may have pushed Simpson over the edge," Darden said. Simpson attended his daughter Sydney's school dance recital that day, an event also attended by Nicole, her mother, and a number of her family members. After the recital, during which Nicole evidently ignored her ex—husband,

Nicole took Sydney and her family—but not Simpson—to the Mezzaluna Trattoria restaurant for a celebration dinner. It was to be the last meal of her life, and the last night Ronald Goldman would work at the restaurant.

Prosecutor Darden then told the jury that Simpson worked himself into a rage because he was spurned by both his ex-wife and his girlfriend at the time, *Vogue* model Paula Barbieri. Then, according to Darden, Simpson formulated a plan to "solve his problems" by killing Ms. Simpson. Darden told the jury, "He always blamed her, and everything was her fault."

In an effort to get the jurors to step into the mind of O. J. Simpson, Darden said that every thrust of the knife into the victims brought Simpson relief from his torment. "With each thrust of that knife into her body and into Ron's body there is a release. . .and he stabs and he cuts and he slices until that rage is gone and until these people are dead. And after that rage is gone, he is better," Darden told the jury. The deputy district attorney claimed that O. J. Simpson was so relieved after committing the violent crimes that he didn't even bother to run away from the crime scene, and he noted that the space between the bloody shoe prints proved that the assailant was walking calmly at the time.

In one of the strongest arguments of the prosecution's case, Darden told the jury that the problems and stresses that culminated in violent murder began long before june 12, 1994. Once again, the prosecutor pointed to the ugly history of physical abuse, battery, and strife that could be traced all the way back to the beginning when Nicole Brown Simpson was still in her teens, and O. J Simpson was the glamorous, and married, professional football star.

From the beginning, the defense team had tried unsuccessfully to have evidence of the Simpsons' turbulent relationship suppressed. This dark side of one of America's most colorful football heroes had been well concealed from the general public until the murder took place in 1994. Darden, a deputy district attorney, co-lead prosecutor in the case, and a respected law school professor, told the jury to get out their Bibles and read the "sixth Proverb" after they returned to their homes. It says, "For jealousy makes a man furious, and he will not spare when he takes revenge" (Prov. 6:34RSV). Then Darden told the jury, "OJ. Simpson is a murderer. You have to look at all the evidence... You'll see that he did it and we proved it. We proved it beyond a rea. sonable doubt."

Once Christopher Darden finished his statements, itwas time for the defense team to take the stage, and when Johnnie Cochran, Jr., stood up to deliver the final summation, he was prepared. Oddly enough, the lead defense attorney spent hours working on his summation with Charles Lindner, a Jewish attorney and a former president of the Criminal Courts Bar Association in Los Angeles, in addition to routine meetings with members of Simpson's own "Dream Team." In statements made to the press later on, Lindner said that during the long hours they spent in re search and discussion, he also told Cochran about his family's experiences in Nazi Germany under Adolf Hitler.

***

It was during this critical week of summations that God began to speak to me about returning to Los Angeles. I didn't know any details, but I felt unusually strongly that the events of September 26th through the 29th would end explosively, and might possibly bring the trial to a rapid and dramatic end somehow. It was so serious that God was telling me to be in Los Angeles on Monday, October 2nd—no matter what the cost. I began to pray for the case with renewed urgency, knowing that whatever the Lord intended to do in this particular trial was quickly coming to a conclusion.

For months I had been praying with johnnie Cochran Jr., every time I went to Los Angeles, and for him countless times each week when. I was in Toronto or elsewhere. I knew from the beginning that he was to play a key role in the trial, and I knew God wanted to do something in his personal life as well. Many times I shared Scripture verses with him. He knew I was praying for O. J. Simpson and every member of the defense team, and he also knew I was praying forjudge Ito, Marcia Clark, Christopher Darden, and the rest of the prosecutors and the jury members. I wasn't in Los Angeles during the two days ofjohnnie Cochran Jr.'s final argument for the defense, but what I learned in the days that followed convinced me he had been listening to my many quotes from Scripture and to Mr. Lindner's memories of a desperate minority struggling to survive under a hostile regime of racial hatred.

***

"If it doesn't fit, you must acquit! "johnnie Cochran, Jr., knew everything he had worked for—including his reputation—was on the line on Wednesday, September 27th. He started his arguments with an unforgettable coined phrase that became a constant reminder of the darkest moment in all of the prosecution's long days in that courtroom. He wanted the jurors to remember the larger-than—life picture of OJ. Simpson apparently struggling unsuccessfully to pull on the shrunken or undersized "bloody glove" while standing in front of the jury box. Prosecutor Christopher Darden would have given almost anything to forget that scene—but even more than that, he wanted the jury to forget it. Cochran quickly made sure that any hope of "forgetfulness" evaporated that day.

From the "no fit, must acquit" argument, Cochran moved on to tackle the prosecution's "timeline" theory and reiterated the defense's position that the murders took place at a later time in the evening than presented by the prosecution. There was definitely room for conjecture; in the absence of any solid forensic proof of the time of death, both sides were forced to rely on howling dogs and the times of "favorite television reruns" of neighborhood witnesses for approximate time markers. Again, all Cochran needed to do was establish "reasonable doubt."

In a classic Cochran move, the lead defense attorney put on a dark knit cap that was very similar to a cap found at the crime scene and asked the jury, "Who am I?" Then he an swered his own question. "I'm Johnnie Cochran with a knit cap on. From two blocks away, O. J. Simpson is O. J. Simpson." The jurors were unlikely to forget Cochran's dramatic visual response to the prosecution claim that O. J. Simpson wore a dark knit cap to disguise himself.

Cochran then showed the jurors a photograph and some video footage of OJ. Simpson taken only a few hours before the murders took place. The trademark smile and happy countenance in those images just did not match the profile of a man about to commit a heinous, premeditated crime, in the defense attorney's opinion. Some legal commentators told national television and radio audiences that Simpson was his own best defense in the courtroom. Throughout the trial, O. J. Simpson "never looked like a killer." He was always impeccably dressed, virtually silent until his statement late in the trial, and self-assured.

Next, Cochran tackled the physical evidence, going to great lengths to keep details to a minimum. He knew that verdicts are decided on an emotional level. Yes, jury panels sometimes agonize over or argue about the evidence, but in the end many jurors essentially "close their eyes" and vote their gut instinct-especially where there is abundant evidence on both sides of a question. He was counting on his hunch that it only takes one or two strong emotional obstacles to derail an entire trainload of evidence.

One of the weakest parts of the prosecution's case against O. J. Simpson was the unusually small amount of blood evidence at his house, most of it questionable according to the defense team. Ifit was true that Simpson had corn mitted the bloody murders, cut his hands in the scuffle with his victims, and walked through pools of blood on his way to the Bronco, then why didn't investigators find abundant blood evidence at Simpson's house? Cochran contended there should have been a great deal of blood found on the light-colored carpet in Simpson's home, as well as on doors and light switches. Cochran also reminded the jurors about the big question that the prosecution had never been able to answer: Why wasn't there blood on the grass and ground cover at the spot the "bloody glove" was found by Detective Mark Fuhrman?

Cochran showed the jurors pictures of O. J. Simpson that were taken by police shortly after his arrest. He pointed out that Simpson was remarkably unscarred and unmarked for a man who supposedly had single-handedly killed two people at once with a knife, especially since one of those alleged victims was a 25-year-old male who was healthy and strong, stood 6' 1", and weighed 171 pounds at the time of his death. The defense attorney said that the attack involved a fierce struggle that should have inflicted a number of wounds on the attacker as well as on the victims. At the very least, there should have been far more wounds than the few cuts Simpson had on his hand at the time of his arrest. Simpson said he got the cuts when reaching for a cellular phone in the Bronco, and from the sharp pieces of a glass he broke in his hand when he received news of his ex-wife's death. Cochran then again attacked the "bloody glove" evidence, but from a different angle. The prosecution had hurriedly recruited the services of Richard Rubin in an attempt to cover their goof in having Simpson unsuccessfully try to put on the "bloody glove" in court. Rubin had testified that the glove was very unique, and that it was the proper size for Simpson. Cochran told the jury that Rubin had given a letter to the prosecutors mentioning something about a "victory party," and bluntly called Rubin a biased witness who was merely "a soldier in the prosecution army."

In his final argument for the day, Cochran switched gears to address O. J. Simpson's past history of physical abuse in his relationship with Nicole Brown Simpson. He emphasized that the incidents were part of his client's dis. tant past and claimed that Simpson had not struck his ex-wife since their much-publicized fight in 1989. "O. J. Simpson is not proud of that 1989 incident. You know what? He paid his debt to that," the attorney said.

Cochran was referring to a New Year's Eve incident that occurred after both of the Simpsons had been drinking. After Simpson struck Nicole, she told the police, "He's going to kill me." That incident led to Simpson's arrest and a court plea of no-contest on a charge of spousal battery. He agreed to pay a fine, do community service, and consented to counseling. Simpson told ESPN that year, "It was embarrassing, but because our relationship was strong and all our friends knew it and they knew what they were reading wasn't necessarily the truth, hey, we just tried to put it behind us and ignore it as much as we could."

When Cochran completed his arguments on Wednesday afternoon, the prosecution must have breathed a sigh of relief. No significant damage had been done to the prosecution case yet; Marcia Clark would have one final salvo to launch just before the jury was sent out for deliberations. Only one more day remained until that point. No one in that courtroom really knew what would happen on Thursday, September 28th, but an emotional lightning rod was about to be raised in "Department 103" that would attract the full fury of a storm of racism that would sweep across the nation.

Part of the way through johnnie Cochran, Jr.'s first day of his closing arguments, his office and the court received a small taste of what the next day would bring. Death threats against Cochran began to come by telephone and later by mail, prompting security guards to totally seal the trial attorneys Wilshire Boulevard offices. Cochran, who had maitained very close ties to the African-American community, made some special security arrangements for the following day (although in the minds of some, there were other motives involved than personal safety).

Those in the courtroom kept waiting for a major attack on Mark Fuhrman and the effect of his blatant racism on the validity of the evidence he gathered against O. J. Simpson, but it did not come. Everyone in the room knew it would come; it was just a matter of time. By the end of the court day on Wednesday, they all knew the answer—Thursday was the day. Few people (if any) could predict the intensity that would propel this argument into the history books, but in a matter of hours, the rest of the world would know.

O. J. Simpson was escorted back to the six-by-nine foot concrete cell in Row G in the Los Angeles County Men's Detention Center that had become his home away from home. The defendant probably wondered how many more days he would spend in his tight quarters courtesy of Los Angeles County. The same facility played host at the time to Erik Menendez, the younger of two brothers accused of murdering their parents in their Beverly Hills home. Menendez was Simpson's only close "neighbor" when he was first arrested, but Menendez was moved five days later after he continued to try to communicate with Simpson. The cell block was host at other times to such notable guests as mass murderer Charles Manson, Richard Ramirez (the Los Angeles "Night Stalker"), and two cousins who jointly were convicted as "the Hillside Stranglers."

The jury was once again escorted back to their secret location at an undisclosed Los Angeles hotel under the supervision of armed guards, and virtually all the major players in the case returned to their homes and offices escorted by sheriff' s deputies, a precaution made necessary by a flurry of death threats. Armed sheriff's deputies were assigned to protect judge Ito, dubbed by the press as "America's most famous judge," when he was targeted by death threats after he decided to limit the number of Fuhrman tape excerpts played before the jury. All three of the surviving sisters of Nicole Brown Simpson were given guards after their lives were threatened, and the leading attorneys on both sides of the case were assigned bodyguards after they received death threats.

CHAPTER 11

Hitler, Fuhrman, and the Bible

The jury wearin trooped into the jury box for another day of seemingly endless arguments about the guilt or innocence of O. J. Simpson in the murders of Nicole Brown Simpson and Ronald Goldman. It was a tough job for $5 a day, even though it provided room and board at a nice hotel and nearly nine months of supervised separation from family and friends. Defense attorneys Johnnie Cochran, Jr., and Barry Scheck were scheduled to present final defense summations that morning, but the dull looks on the faces of the jury members would make most trial attorneys wish they had chosen another profession.

There was no reason for the jurors to expect anything new that morning. (Of course, they hadn't seen johnnie Cochran, Jr., arrive at the Criminal Courts Building that day Hanked by six tall, stern bodyguards dressed in the distinctive bright bow ties, pressed suits, and white shirts common to members of the Nation of Islam, also known as Black Muslims.) The rules of the game said that no new evidence could be presented in summaries, and as the saying goes, "Old news is no news." It looked like everyone in the courtroom that day was facing just another compressed rehash of old defense arguments countering old prosecution arguments. Then johnnie Cochran, Jr., rose from his seat with the defense team to the right of Judge Lance Ito and appreached the jury of ten women and two men (including nine African-Americans).

Cochran knew his arguments the day before had been effective, but he also knew the defense team hadn't won the war yet. There was still a mountain of circumstantial evidence stacked against his client, but he was about to light the fuse on some explosive arguments that would be heard around the world. He felt confident he could free his client now, but he was uneasy about the aftershocks he knew would follow...

The topic was racism, Mark Fuhrman-style, andjohnnie Cochran, Jr., tackled his subject with the power and passion of a tent revival preacher in front of a capacity crowd. Sure, there was a mountain of evidence, but the lead defense attorney "stood atop that mountain" and pointed his finger at the two detectives responsible for producing much of that evidence the day after the murders. He told the jurors that De tective Philip Vannatter was Fuhrman's ally, and that he was the "man who carried the blood" in their planned attempt to frame O. J. Simpson. Vannatter's strange departure from established police procedure in deciding to carry Simpson's blood sample in his pocket from police headquarters to Simpson's estate the day of the murders "showed he was in on the conspiracy." The blood sample, which was taken from O. J. Simpson's veins the day after the murders, should have been immediately booked into evidence for safekeeping and proper storage by the police lab. Instead, it took an unauthorized ride in Vannatter's coat pocket to Simpson's estate where LAPD criminologists were combing the scene for evidence. In Cochran's mind the implication was obvious: Vannatter's action strongly suggested evidence-planting.

Calling Fuhrman and Vannatter "the twin devils of deception," Cochran pressed hard to prove that Fuhrman's long-held and well-documented hatred of blacks, jews, and interracial marriages tainted everything he did-including his police work. His overriding prejudice contaminated everything he touched—including the so—called evidence pre sented against O. J. Simpson.

When the double murders occurred, Fuhrman saw his chance to finally make "the big arrest" he was always looking for, according to Cochran. It was when the detective learned in the 1980's that Simpson, an African-American Hall of Fame football star, was married to a white woman, that he targeted Simpson. "A racist is someone who has power over you. This man would lie and set you up because of the hatred he has in his heart!" Cochran claimed that when Nicole Brown Simpson and Ronald Goldman were found slain, it gave F uhrman a once-in-a-lifetime chance to plant evidence without detection and frame Simpson for first—degree murder.

Observers in the courtroom said the jury sat transfixed by the lead defense counsel's thundering delivery. Cochran played the tape recording of F uhrman uttering the same shocking racial epithet that he had sworn to the jury he had not used in a decade. Then Cochran read each word of a letter from Kathleen Bell, who testified earlier that Fuhrman told her he thought all blacks should be gathered together and "burned." OJ. Simpson's lead attorney told the members of the jury that fate had given them a chance to change history, saying, "Maybe there's a reason why we're here. Maybe you're the right people at the right time at the right place to say: 'No more!' Stop this cover-up! Stop this cover-up! You are the consciences of this community." He urged the jury to "do the right thing" and acquit Simpson as a way to send a message to the world that racism and police misconduct would not be tolerated.

The most controversial portion of Cochran's argument came when he made a direct comparison between Detective Mark Fuhrman and Adolf Hitler, the demented German dictator whose race-motivated hatred and extreme ethnic pride sparked a world war that engulfed entire continents and killed millions. Hitler personally ordered the mass genocide of Jews, Poles, the retarded, and homosexuals, labeling them all as defective, and blaming them for society's ills.

Knowing this was his last opportunity to speak to the jury before they would deliver a verdict, Cochran boldly asked them to acquit OJ. Simpson. He spoke of his client's love for his two children by Nicole, his daughter Sydney and his son justin. Then Cochran stood in front of a wall-size photographic image of Simpson with little Sydney, and said, "Someone has taken these children's mother. I hope your decision doesn't take their father."

Cochran summarized his arguments that day with "15 Points for Reasonable Doubt" (reproduced verbatim, for the most part, below). Each question or statement in the list was engineered to produce one thing and one thing only in the minds of the jurors: *doubt.* Cochran urged the 12 jurors to ask themselves these 15 questions as they considered "reasonable doubt" in the accusations made against O. J. Simpson:

1. Why. . .did the blood show up on the sock almost two months after a careful search for evidence? And why, as demonstrated by Dr. [Henry] Lee and Professor [Herbert] MacDonell, was the blood applied when there was no foot in it?

2. Why was Mark Fuhrman, a detective who had been pushed off the case, the person who went by himself to the Bronco, over the fence to interrogate Kato to discover the glove and the thump, thump, thump area?

3. Why was the glove still moist when Fuhrman found it if Mr. Simpson had dropped it. seven hours earlier?

4. If Mark Fuhrman. . .would speak so openly about hi intense genocidal racism to a relative stranger such as Kathleen Bell, how many of his co-workers, the other detectives in this case, were also aware that he lied when he denied using "the n-word," yet failed to come forward?

5. Why did the prosecution not call a single police officer to rebut police photographer [Rolf] Rokahr's testimony that Detective Fuhrman was pointing at the glove before, before Fuhrman went to Rockingham? (That is around 4:30 in the morning.)

6. If the glove had been dropped on the walkway at Rockingham 10 minutes after the murder, why is there no blood or fiber on that south walkway or on the leaves the glove was resting on? Why is there no blood in the 150 feet of narrow walkway, on the stucco walk abutting it?

7. For what purpose was [LAPD Detective] Vannatter carrying Mr. Simpson's blood in his pocket for three hours and a distance of 25 miles instead of booking it down the hall at Parker Center?

8. Why did Deputy District Attorney Hank Goldberg, in a desperate effort to cover up for the missing 1.5 milliliters of Mr. Simpson's blood, secretly go out to the home of police nurse Thano Peratis without notice to the defense and get him to contradict his previous sworn testimony at both the grand jury and the preliminary hearing?

9. Why, if according to Ms. Clark, he walked into his own house wearing the murder clothes and shoes is there not any soil or so much as a smear or drop of blood associated with the victims

on the floor, the white carpeting, the doorknobs, the light switches, and his bedding?

10. If Mr. Simpson had just killed Mr. Goldman in a bloody battle involving more than two dozen knife wounds—where Mr. Goldman remained standing and struggling for several minutes—how come there is less than seven-tenths of one drop of blood consistent with Mr. Goldman found in the Bronco?

11. Why, following a bitter struggle alleged with Mr. Goldman was there no bruises or marks on O. J. Simpson's body?

12. Why do bloodstains with the most DNA not show up until weeks after the murders?

13. Why did Mark Fuhrman lie to us?

14. Why did Phil Vannatter lie to us?

15. Given Professor MacDonell's testimony that the gloves would not have shrunk no matter how much blood was smeared on them, and given that they never shrank onjune 21, 1994, until now despite being repeatedly frozen and thawed, how come the gloves just don't fit?

Cochran quoted Frederick Douglas, a nineteenth century African-American leader and statesman; Cicero, a Roman statesman, orator, and author from the first century BC; and Abraham Lincoln. He also cited passages from the Book of Proverbs stating that false witnesses must be punished, and he urged the jurors to carry out God's will. Finally he stepped up his delivery to an even higher level of intensity and urged the jurors to become soldiers in a fight against racism, saying, "You and I, fighting for freedom and ideals and for justice for all, must continue to expose hate and genocidal racism and these tendencies. We, then," he told the jury, "become the guardians of the Constitution." Finally, Cochran concluded his passionate appeal to the jury by saying, "I know you will stay the course, keep your eye on the prize, and do the right thing [a general reference to Philippians 3:13-14 and First Corinthians 9:24]. God bless you."

When Cochran finally ended his part of the defense arguments for the day, judge Lance Ito told the jurors that Deputy District Attorney Marcia Clark would conclude her rebuttal on Friday (the next day), clearing the way for the 12 month-old trial to be turned over to them for a final verdict. Observers noticed that the dazed jury didn't seem to respond to the judge's news. They were just trying to get through the day.

Not everyone was thrilled with johnnie Cochran, Jr.'s oratory that day. Throughout Cochran's presentation, Fred Goldman, the father of Ronald Goldman, was visibly agitated. During the break, Goldman could contain his anger no longer. He walked straight into the TV lights of eager journalists and released his bitter response to the defense attorney's statements:

"This man is sick!" Goldman declared. "This man is a horror walking around amongst us. We have seen a man who perhaps is the worst kind of racist himself, someone who shoves racism in front of everything, someone who compares a person who speaks racist comments to Hitler, a person who murdered millions of people. This man is the worst kind of human being imaginable." Referring to Cochran's appearance that morning accompanied by bodyguards from Louis Farrakhan's Nation of Islam, Goldman angrily asked reporters, "He's talking about racism, and he's talking about hate? Who does he connect himself with? This man ought to be ashamed of himself to walk among decent human beings." Cochran's response to Fred Goldman's comments to the media was to say that it is corruption on the lowest levels that permits men like Hitler to come to power.

O. J. Simpson's family members had generally avoided making comments to the media, but Fred Goldman's comments spurred them to hastily call their own press conference. Simpson's sister, Carmelita Simpson-Dario, told reporters, "We have waited all this time, and now. . .the attorneys are telling my brother's story. And it's very shocking that once johnnie gets up and starts telling what we feel happened that this has rocked somebody's world." Her sister Shirley Baker, flanked in front of the microphones by Simpson's two grown children and his mother, told the media, "It's wrong, even when you're hurting, for someone to get up and personally attack our lawyers and say they're liars."

Outside the court, LAPD Detective Tom Lange (who was an investigator on the Simpson case with Detective Philip Vannatter), criticized Cochran's passionate appeal to the jury, telling reporters, "The preacher has turned into a snake oil salesman."

Many legal observers hired by major media networks covering the trial were surprised when defense attorney Barry Scheck stood to deliver the second and final series of arguments for the defense team that afternoon. Originally brought to the team for his nationally recognized expertise in the use of DNA evidence based on "genetic fingerprinting" techniques in criminal trials, Scheck's no-nonsense cross-examination ability had brought him to the front of the pack as the trial progressed. His cooler, scientific analysis of the DNA evidence at the core of the prosecution case was seen as a perfect counterpoint to Cochran's impassioned arguments against the racial prejudice he claimed had poisoned the police investigation from the start.

Scheck told the jurors, "There is a cancer at the heart of this case," and claimed that all the prosecution's DNA evidence against 0. J. Simpson was untrustworthy because it was based on blood samples that were contaminated and tampered with in the "black hole" of the Los Angeles Police Department crime lab. He bluntly told the 12 jurors, "Somebody played with this evidence. There's no doubt about it."

Then he recalled an analogy mentioned by Dr. Henry Lee, one of the most respected expert witnesses called by the defense. Dr. Lee had compared the discovery of faulty evidence in the prosecution's case to discovering a cockroach in a bowl of spaghetti—if you find one, the whole bowl is probably infested. "How many cockroaches do you have to find in the bowl of spaghetti?" Scheck asked the jury. "This is reasonable doubt."

After attorneys promised judge Ito that they would end all arguments on Friday early enough for the judge to give his final instructions to the jury, and for the jury to select a foreperson, he recessed court three hours early. He announced that deliberations would begin the following week on Monday.

As the courtroom began to empty, shock waves from the day's arguments began to ripple across the nation and around the world. President Bill Clinton, who watched part of the proceedings from the White House in Washington, DC, told the media he was concerned that the case was becoming symbolic of racial issues. The President, who played golf with O. J. Simpson just three weeks before the murders, also criticized the "circus atmosphere" surrounding the double-murder case. Mr. Clinton, who had served as Arkansas' Attorney General for two years prior to being elected governor of that state, blamed live television coverage for feeding the "press frenzy" in Los Angeles. Although he felt that all criminal trials should be open to the public and the media, he opposed having television cameras in the courtroom, saying "...you run the risk of having more derailments and distractions if you have televised trials."

Spokesmen for the Anti-Defamation League, a jewish civil rights organization, publicly condemned lead defense attorney johnnie Cochran, Jr.'s reference to Adolf Hitler in his closing statements. They felt it was entirely inappropriate to compare the personal racist views of a LAPD detective with the carefully engineered genocide conducted against Jews in World War II by the Nazi dictator and his army.

Rabbi Abraham Cooper of the Simon Wiesenthal Center, a privately flmded agency founded to carry on the work of Wiesenthal, the famous "Nazi hunter," also publicly condemned Cochran's comparison of Adolf Hitler's genocidal programs that killed millions of civilian jews in the Holocaust of World War II with Mark Fuhrman's racist views.

The rabbi also said, "We are shocked that Johnnie Cochran has enveloped himself in the Nation of Islam" (referring to Cochran's new guardians wearing bright bow ties). "My question to Johnnie Cochran," Rabbi Cooper told the media, "would be how would he feel if the prosecution surrounded themselves with neo-Nazis and skinheads to get into the courthouse?"

Defense attorney Robert Shapiro was also deeply offended by the direction of defense colleague Johnnie Cochran, Jr.'s final arguments, and especially by the reference to Adolf Hitler. During preliminary hearings before O. J. Simpson's arrest, and before Shapiro was moved aside as lead attorney, the respected Jewish attorney told the media, "Race is not and will not be an issue in this defense. The only thing we are looking at is credibility of witnesses." His old friend, F. Lee Bailey, opposed Shapiro's defense strategy from the beginning. He wanted to portray Mark Fuhrman as a racist to discredit his testimony months before the "Fuhrman tapes" surfaced, and Johnnie Cochran, Jr., agreed. Many observers felt this fundamental disagreement led to Shapiro's demotion on the team, even though he was the man who assembled the "Dream Team" in the first place.

TV commentators and legal experts began to make comments about "playing the race card" and "jury nullification" when referring to Cochran's emotional arguments urging the jury to take a proactive role against racism. They feared the attorney's plea would encourage the jury to vote "along color lines" without regard to justice or to the evidence presented in the case, but Cochran claimed he had not "played the race card."

***

Thousand of miles to the east and north in Toronto, I was praying for the OJ. Simpson trial in Los Angeles. The airline tickets for Roxanne and I were purchased on Wednesday, and we had already made plans to leave for Los Angeles for arrival on Monday, October 2nd. The case was coming to a rapid and emotional conclusion, and I had received "my marching orders" from God. For some reason, I had to be there by Monday morning. It seemed highly unlikely that anything could happen by then; after all, the court case had drug on for almost a year. Surely the jury would require a considerable amount of time to wade through all that testimony and evidence. Nevertheless, I would be there Monday as ordered.

Meanwhile, I knew things had reached a fever pitch in Los Angeles. I was a bit shocked by some of the news I saw on television. Was it really necessary for Johnnie Cochran, Jr., to travel around town with six of Farrakhan's bodyguards? What did Robert Shapiro think about Cochran's reference to Adolf Hitler? Was it wise for him to appeal to the jury on racial grounds? All I knew was that God had a greater plan for this trial that totally overshadowed the outcome of the verdict.

I knew in my heart that God was on the scene and that settled the matter for me. Even if the unthinkable should occur—if a guilty man was set free or an innocent man found guilty—I knew God would have His way in everything. In my view, and just as strongly in the mind of Rev. Smith, all of us are guilty people who have been allowed to walk free. Yet all of us will face a personal accounting from a Supreme Judge who needs no witnesses, expert testimony, or evidence exhibits. He knows all, and the Bible implies that we will all be judged by the very words we've spoken and the deeds we've done (see Mt. 12:36-37; Lk. 19:22). Our innocence and freedom come because Jesus Christ, the one innocent man and the Son of God, chose to take our punishment in our place.

For my part, I was to remain totally neutral—no matter how I felt about the individuals I met, or how they received or rejected me. I was not to be swayed by evidence or argument; my assignment and duty was to pray and to keep on praying until God's will was worked out in the trial in front of the nation. I had the distinct impression He was out to restore justice to a nation through the events of this trial— whether it was through a nationally telen'sed act of justice or of injustice in the courts. Friday was to be the beginning of the end, and I ended the day on Thursday on my knees.

CHAPTER 12

The Verdict

Once again, the 12 members of the jury in the OJ. Simpson double—murder trial braced themselves for the emotional trauma of "the photos." Deputy District Attorney Marcia Clark was winding up her final rebuttal to the arguments of defense attorneys Johnnie Cochran, Jr., and Barry Scheck, and she had to go to her strongest images to revive the exhausted jury.

As the distraught family members of Nicole Brown Simpson and Ronald Goldman fought back a fresh flood of tears, Clark replayed the haunting 911 tape recordings and flashed a photo of Nicole Brown Simpson's savagely beaten face. They record the incident on New Year's Day in 1989 when Nicole's husband beat her after finding a picture of an old boyfriend in her picture album. That beating sent Nicole to the hospital and O. J. Simpson to a courtroom where he pled no-contest to charges of spousal battery.

The tears continued to flow in the gallery with renewed sobs as the lead prosecutor flashed a seven-foot high image of Ron Goldman's bloody body crumpled just off the walkway leading to Nicole's Brentwood condominium. "Usually, I feel I'm the only one left to speak for the victims," Clark said as she glanced at the lurid photo and then peered into the faces of the weary jurors. "But Nicole and Ron are speaking to you." Recalling testimony submitted long ago when the trial was young, Clark urged the 12 jurors to remember and consider what Nicole told a police detective who responded to her domestic violence call in 1988: "He's going to kill me."

Despite almost continuous defense objections from johnnie Cochran, Jr., and Barry Scheck (a total of 60 were made in the course of her arguments), Ms. Clark continued to press the central points of her case. She replayed another crucial 911 tape recording—this one made only eight months before the murders—of the frightened voice of Nicole Brown Simpson begging the police to protect her from her ex—husband. The angry voice of O. J. Simpson could be plainly heard raging in the background.

The defense team was upset over Clark's repeated re plays of the 911 tapes, and accused her of putting on "a production" that unfairly mingled unrelated evidence for maximum emotional effect, but Judge Ito allowed her to continue. Prosecutor Clark made the most of her opportunity. While the 911 tapes filled the courtroom with Nicole's haunting pleas for help, Clark flashed a series of images on the large projection screen and Nicole's surviving sisters, Tanya and Denise Brown, covered their ears and cried with their mother, Juditha Brown. The jurors saw a montage of scenes, including Ms. Simpson's beaten face in 1989, the crime scene, blood drops on O. J. Simpson's driveway, Simpson's white Bronco, a bloody glove, and finally, the ghastly police photograph taken on june 13, 1994, of the victims' slashed bodies huddled at the enclosed entrance to Nicole's home.

Marcia Clark told the jurors that Ron Goldman was a hero. 'Ron, struggling so valiantly, forced the killer to leave evidence."

Clark then looked at the jury and said, "They told you with their blood, with their hair..." Then she turned in mid-sentence to face O. J. Simpson who sat expressionless at the counsel table, and continued her sentence in one smooth motion, "...that he did it—Orenthal Simpson." The tension in the courtroom was magnified as Clark once again allowed the victims to speak for themselves through video-tape and pictures. Then she made her final appeal to the jury of ten women and two men, urging them to find a national sports legend guilty of murdering his ex—wife and her friend. Then it was over.

There would be no more arguments, conferences at the bench, exhibits entered, witnesses called, or motions made. Judge Lance Ito turned toward the jury as the prosecutor took her seat, and he reminded the jury that it was their sworn duty to "reach a just verdict regardless of the consequences." He knew that thoughts about the growing crowds outside the courtroom, and possibly lingering memories of the race riots that struck Los Angeles during the Rodney King beating incident, could easily influence the weary jury members.

The Superior Court judge had another concern too. "You are not partisans or advocates, but impartial judges of the facts," Ito instructed the jurors in a pointed rebuff of some of the arguments presented on the previous day. Finally, he ordered the jury of nine African-Americans, two whites, and one Hispanic, to ignore previous cautions by lawyers that "the world is watching." Then the judge delivered the case into their hands. Twelve anonymous people now held the future of OJ. Simpson in their hands. By law, if justice was to be served, it would be because they made the right decision.

After he delivered his final instructions, judge Ito told the 12 jurors to move into the jury room and elect a foreperson. The jury left the courtroom at 4:08 pm. while the judge, counsel for both sides, and spectators waited. There was still a pervading tension in the room, a leftover by product of the tragic images and voices witnessed earlier that day. At 4:11, only three minutes after the jury filed out of the courtroom, a jury room buzzer sounded three times in a row, jolting the people waiting in the courtroom. It was a signal that the jury had already selected a foreperson. The shocked silence was fractured by Johnnie Cochran, Jr.'s quick remark, "Maybe they've got a verdict and we can all go home." Laughter suddenly filled the room and drove away the grim tension—for a moment, at least. Now the jury would retire without beginning formal deliberations, despite their willingness to "work nights and weekends" to press through to a timely verdict. In a trial that had endured almost every kind of delay imaginable, a new one had managed to intervene in the twelfth hour—the entire court building was closed that afternoon, all weekend, and for half the day Monday for electrical repairs. The jury was told they would begin deliberations at noon on Monday, October 2nd.

Outside the courtroom on Temple Street nine stories below, police ofiicers sensed a sudden turn in the mood of the swelling crowds. With hundreds of portable television sets and radios in the crowd, the spectators knew the exact moment the jury was dismissed, and that was when the carnival-like mood on the street suddenly became more serious, and almost grim.

Frank Ramirez, a spokesman for the Los Angeles Police Department, announced to the media that the department was cracking down to enforce tighter crowd control in front of the courthouse. The move was a rapid response to the ominous change in the crowd when the jury was dismissed. The police blocked off the Temple Street entrance and posted notices saying it was closed to the public until further notice from 7:00 am. to 10:00 am, and from 7 :00 pm. until the last attorney working on the OJ. Simpson murder case had left the premises. Ramirez told reporters, "We don't want anyone to get hurt."

The day had started off in a totally different way. That morning, the crowds gathered quickly and were even more colorful and demonstrative than usual, but the people were more jovial and friendly at first. Many of the spectators actually cheered when the defense attorneys arrived at the Criminal Courts Building, especially when they saw lead defense attorney Johnnie Cochran, Jr., emerge from his vehicle, accompanied by his extremely conspicuous retinue of six tall Black Muslim bodyguards, complete with bright bow ties and stem looks.

The mood was congenial even inside the courthouse that morning. Just before the morning session began, Juditha Brown, Nicole's mother, walked over to O. J. Simpson's mother, Eunice, who was seated in a wheelchair due to arthritis and a heart condition, and gently kissed her on the cheek. Despite the painful events of the previous year, the two women had built a warm relationship during the decade, and more they had shared as mothers-in-law for Nicole and O. J. They both knew that regardless of the outcome of the criminal court case involving O. J. Simpson, there were two innocent grandchildren who clearly loved and desperately needed both of their grandmothers.

***

About midday on Friday in Toronto, I could almost sense a turning or twist in the spiritual climate in Los Angeles. I knew in my heart that something significant had just happened in the OJ. Simpson case, and the spiritual climate had been dramatically altered. When I talked with Rev. Smith about his impressions of the situation in Los Angeles, he immediately agreed with me and said the mood change was something almost tangible.

Rev. Smith told me that he felt the mood had almost turned ugly. A harsh edge had converted the carnival atmosphere on the streets around the courthouse to one of malignancy. He almost felt like the court was being "held hostage," or at the very least was the pawn at the center of a massive struggle between incredible forces. I was sure that, even though the members of the jury were being carefully shielded from news reports and from public contact of any kind, they could still feel or somehow sense the incredible pressure mounted against them in the spirit realm.

I told Rev. Smith that I was also deeply concerned about the attorneys involved in the trial. Nearly every one of them had lost something as a direct result of the trial. I was deeply concerned about Marcia Clark, whose personal life was nearly in shambles by the time she stood to deliver her final rebuttal that Friday. I sensed that she felt like "the accused" herself. Her private life, her failures, and her fears had been dragged onto front pages and prime time newscasts on a weekly basis for months. She had been unfairly labeled as a bad mother, a hysterical woman, a domineering female, and an overly ambitious deputy district attorney who would do almost anything to win her case. All along, the Holy Spirit told me she was a hurting woman with a broken heart who desperately needed to find an anchor for her life. She was talented, intelligent, articulate, and yes, ambitious, but above all, she had become very lonely.

Christopher Darden was a brilliant attorney with a gentle heart. He had made a major mistake with the "bloody glove" incident in which O. J. Simpson was apparently unable to pull on the glove found at the crime scene. Some critics thought Darden's blunder might cost the prosecution every— thing in the O. J. Simpson case. Darden won the respect of the critics with his excellent performance during the summations, but regardless of the outcome, he had lost faith in the judicial system. After several grueling months on the O. J. Simpson case, he had said publicly that he might never prosecute another case.

Johnnie Cochran, Jr., seemed to be reaching for every "helpful straw" he could find, regardless of the strings attached or the possible repercussions they may create. In an effort to sway the jury in favor of his "racist conspiracy" theory in the O. J. Simpson case, he may have stirred up a storm of racism and separatism that no one but God could calm again. Some feared that his courtroom tactics had permanently damaged the ability of American juries to function independently and without prejudice. I continued to pray earnestly for him, for God had made it clear that He had a higher plan for Johnnie Cochran, Jr.

F. Lee Bailey was also on my heart, though he was never very open to prayer or input from me. My job was to pray, regardless of the reception I received. From the beginning, Mr. Bailey wanted to picture Mark Fuhrman as a racist, and he dually had his way. In the process, he lost an old friend in Robert Shapiro, and forever changed the complexion of the court system in which he made his living.

Robert Shapiro weighed especially heavy on my heart. This respected Jewish attorney had made it clear from the beginning that he despised the "racial approach" to defending his client, O. J. Simpson. As the lead attorney who engineered and pulled together the "Dream Team" to defend OJ. Simpson, he publicly promised not to pursue "the race card" at the very beginning of the case. But johnnie Cochran, Jr., joined the team and his overpowering personality and flamboyant style quickly brought him to the head of the team.

When Shapiro's fellow "Dream Team" attorneys decided to shift gears toward the racist conspiracy defense later in the case, he was demoted to number three on the team as F. Lee Bailey moved up one slot. I learned later that Shapiro refused to go along when the "Dream Team" went to lunch together on the Friday the jury selected its foreperson. He was still angry over johnnie Cochran, Jr.'s decision to compare Mark Fuhrman with Adolf Hitler in summary arguments the day before, with the troop of Black Muslim bodyguards he now traveled with, and with other key differences that had come to a head between Shapiro, Bailey, and Cochran on Thursday.

I mentioned earlier that the Lord had warned me in advance about a major change in the case. I didn't have any specifics at first—I just knew I was supposed to be in Los Angeles by Monday morning. No one knew just how quickly the case would come to a conclusion. The media knew that both sides were to close their cases on Friday, but no one knew how quickly the jury would act once they began deliberations. I made travel arrangements on Wednesday, but I couldn't get a flight out to Los Angeles until very early Monday morning, the second of October-the same morning the Lord told me to be in Los Angeles.

When Friday came around, I knew by the Spirit that the case would be decided on Monday. It seemed impossible, but when I confirmed that both sides had rested their cases on Friday, I was convinced I had heard from God. If I didn't have confirmation before I reached the airport, I certainly had it afterward. At that time there were no direct flights from Toronto to Los Angeles. Therefore, since my flight was technically an international flight with multiple connections, I had be checked in and ready to board my 1:00 am. flight by midnight. When I arrived at the airport, I was told the airliner I was scheduled to board developed mechanical problems and the flight had to be canceled! I thought, "Lord, You told me to be in Los Angeles today. I've done everything I know to do help me get to California in time." Somehow I ended up being transferred by Northwest Airlines to a 4:30 Air Canada flight (which also ended up running one and a half hours late). So it wasn't easy to get to Los Angeles on Monday, October 2nd.

Rev. Smith arrived at the Los Angeles International Airport early Monday morning expecting to pick me up for a routine trip to my hotel. He walked into the airport and started looking for me, only to notice flashing flight schedule screens saying my flight was canceled. He knew how important this trip was, and he began to make calls to every airline he could think of. At first he thought I might still be in Toronto, but eventually he tracked me down to the Air Canada flight somehow.

Since my flight delays had brought me to Los Angeles so late, we went directly from the airport to the Criminal Courts Building—only to discover that the entire courthouse building had been sealed off from the public. Police squad cars were blocking each end of Temple Street fronting the building, and we saw 10 to 15 officers standing by the cruisers to make sure no one slipped by. No spectators were being admitted to the courtroom—in fact, they weren't even allowed in the Criminal Courts Building on Monday and Tuesday because the authorities were deeply concerned over the rising possibility of violence occurring when the verdict was announced.

I knew God told me He wanted me to be in place in the courthouse on Monday morning, and I trusted Him to make a way as He had done so often before. Of course I firmly believe that prayer is unaffected by distance, but I also know that God always has very specific and often hidden reasons for placing us in certain physical locations at certain times. That particular morning, He wanted me inside that sealed courthouse (even though hundreds of armed police officers had orders to keep me and everyone else out).

Again, the grace of God preceded us. Although Temple Street had been blockaded and the larger-than-usual crowds were restricted to specific areas behind police barriers, God Worked a major miracle for us that day. One of our friends with the Los Angeles County Sheriff's Department hap-pened to be getting out of his car near us and we struck up a conversation with him as he began to walk toward the courthouse building.

Although we didn't plan it that way, we just kept talking about our assignment and the sheriff's deputy just kept listening and walking toward the courthouse building. We walked and talked past the police barriers, past the armed guards at the door, and right past the security forces in the lobby. The officers with the sheriff's department and the Los Angeles Police Department must of thought we were "with him" because they allowed us through the security lines and through the courthouse door without a challenge. We asked our friend about staying in the building to pray that day and during the court proceedings on Tuesday. He told us that he thought Sheriff Block, who had come to know us well in previous months, wouldn't mind if we would stay in the cafeteria. We just had to stay out of the way and remain in the cafeteria until it was all over!

****

The Los Angeles County Sheriff's Department was determined to be ready for any situation once the OJ. Simpson case was turned over to the jury. Sheriff Sherman Block told the media he was looking for a "major outpouring" no matter which way the verdict went. "There will be protest or celebration, depending on your point of view," he said. He also said he would put his 7,OOO-man force on "tactical alert" whenever a verdict seemed imminent. That meant that all on—duty personnel were to be ready for immediate response in the case of an emergency.

The Los Angeles Police Department assigned two platoons of its elite Metro Division along with mounted police to assist the security officers already assigned to the area around the Criminal Courts Building. (Late on Monday, the morning shift of the LAPD was ordered to stay on duty past their usual times long enough for the verdict to be announced to the public on Tuesday, which doubled the number of police officers normally on duty citywide. The number of day shift officers was increased by one third.)

Police authorities blocked off Temple Street, along with Rockingham Avenue (which passes in front of OJ. Simpson's estate) and Bundy Drive (in front of Nicole Brown Simpson's condo) to all vehicle and spectator foot traffic. Officials also established a central command center in the basement of City Hall, which was staffed with police and fire command personnel for emergency operations and interagency coordination.

Attendance in the courtroom was limited to a bare skeleton crew Monday afternoon. The jury began its deliberations at noon, and besides a few hard-core media representatives, the key people in the courtroom consisted of OJ. Simpson and defense attorney Carl Douglas, the African-American barrister who helped present opening arguments early in the case; and prosecutor Christopher Darden. Marcia Clark, Johnnie Cochran, Jr., Robert Shapiro, and F. Lee Bailey were waiting for news in other locations, as were family members of the accused and the victims. No one really expected to hear anything for several days.

Douglas, Simpson, and Darden were there as official witnesses whenever the jury requested "readbacks," in which portions of testimony were read back to the jury to clarify specific issues or incidents. The jurors spent only about an hour of their deliberation time listening to testimony by limousine driver Allan Park's descriptions of phone calls he'd made to his boss, and of his efforts to rouse somebody at O. J. Simpson's house on the night of the murders by ringing a bell at the front gate.

The message came without warning. Only four hours after the jury began its deliberations Monday afternoon, Judge Lance Ito was surprised by a message from the jury forewoman. They had a verdict! When he summoned the jury to the courtroom, two-thirds of the seats in the gallery were empty and the two leading attorneys in the case weren't even there. Most of the media had been caught off guard. They were still passing time upstairs in the pressroom when judge Ito asked the forewoman, "Is that correct?" referring to their arriving at a unanimous verdict. She said, "Yes," and history was made.

Several people in the courtroom gasped, and virtually everyone was shocked. Simpson and Carl Douglas were stunned. Afterward, Douglas said, "Surprise doesn't begin to describe my feelings." Darden was equally surprised. When he was asked if he could believe the jury had reached a verdict so quickly, he said, "I think I have to believe it. It's happening. Nothing shocks me anymore."

In keeping with the ongoing tradition of this trial, a mixup even intruded on this brief interaction in the courtroom. When the jury forewoman told judge Ito the jury had reached a verdict, he asked her for the verdict forms she was supposed to fill out and deliver with her announcement. Embarrassed, she admitted that she had left them inside a sealed envelope in the deliberation room. "That's not a very good place for it," Ito said, and sent her to retrieve the envelope in the company of a court bailiff.

Before the jury was dismissed prior to deliberations the week before, judge Ito had promised the attorneys for both sides in the case that he would provide four hours of prior notice before bringing the jury into the courtroom to announce a verdict. So after he had the sealed envelope containing the verdict forms in his hands, judge Ito explained that the verdict would not be opened and read until 10 o'clock the next morning so attorneys and other observers would have time to be in the courtroom for the announcement. Then he told the jurors, "Ladies and gentle men, have your last pleasant evening," O. J. Simpson stood once again, knowing he would have to spend at least one more night in his cell before he would learn his fate.

On Tuesday, October 3rd, the gallery in "Department 103" was packed. History was in the making and everyone in that room knew it. Outside, the police had been busy since early that morning when the crowds began to gather even earlier than usual. The news media had announced to the world that "the verdict" would be read that morning, and in many places normal activity came to a halt.

As Hurricane Opal descended in fury on the beachfronts of Pensacola, Florida, many residents there were reluctant to tear themselves away from their TV sets, afraid they would miss "the verdict." In fact, so many delayed their flight from the killer storm that government authorities advised the tardy residents to give up trying to flee the storm. They advised those stuck in the path of the storm to stay home and wait it out (in front of their TV sets, of course).

While the roar of news helicopters and restless crowds filled the streets outside the Criminal Courts Building that Tuesday morning, a tense quiet filled the room as Superior Courtjudge Lance Ito asked OJ. Simpson to stand and face the jury while the jury panel's verdict was read on the two counts of first-degree murder in the case of *The People versus Orenthaljames Simpson.* Everyone in the courtroom seemed to hold their breath. Then two words were heard: "Not guilty."

Those words were being broadcast live around the world via satellite, and the people gathered on the street below and in cities and homes across the world exploded in a deafening cacophony of sound. Some were rejoicing in ecstasy, and some were weeping in sorrow or rage.

The greatest contrast was seen in the courtroom itself. The day before, Ron Goldman's younger sister, Kim Goldman, was waiting by the phone for any news about a jury verdict. She was the first to hear about the quick verdict, and she told the media on Monday as she fought back tears, "I have faith in the jury, that they'll do the right thing, to find this beast [Simpson] guilty." On Tuesday, she was seated with family members near the front of the spectator section when the verdict was read. In an instant her hopes were destroyed and she pressed her head to her father's chest and cried out, "Oh my God! N—o—o—o!" Fred Goldman sat back in his seat in disbelief at first, then he embraced his daughter. Finally, he lowered his head in his hands and moaned.

When the verdict was read and the jury panel dismissed, O. J. Simpson looked toward the members of the jury and silently mouthed the words, "Thank you" while motionng to them with his hand. Judge Lance Ito ordered the bailiff to take Simpson to the Sheriff's Department and release him immediately, and Simpson turned to hug his lead defense attorney, Johnnie Cochran, Jr., and his friend and attorney Robert Kardashian.

Simpson's family members were smiling and wiping away tears, waiting to hug O. J. and his son, jason, sat in his seat still sobbing in relief. Prosecutors Marcia Clark and Christopher Darden sat in their seats without expression- they had nothing more to give or say.

Anxious reporters raced one another from one subject to another, hoping for the most shocking response to the verdict. Fred Goldman was a study in outrage and frustration. The father of a young man who was killed because he happened to be "at the wrong place at the wrong time," he was sure O. J. Simpson was his son's killer. He told reporters, "This prosecution team did not lose today. I deeply believe this country lost today. Justice was not served."

O. J. Simpson issued a statement that was read by his son, Jason, during a courthouse news conference also attended by other family members and defense lawyers. The statement said:

"I'm relieved that this part of the incredible nightmare that occurred onJune 12, 1994, is over. My first obligation is to my young children, who will be raised the way that Nicole and I had always planned. My second obligation is to my family and to those friends who never wavered in their support.

"But when things have settled a bit, I will pursue as my primary goal in life the killer or killers who slaughtered Nicole and Mr. Goldman. They are out there somewhere. Whatever it takes to identify them and bring them in, I will provide somehow.

"I can only hope that someday, despite every prejudicial thing that has been said about me publicly, both in and out of the courtroom, people will come to understand and believe that I would not, could not, and did not kill anyone."

***

Rev. Smith and I were about to leave the building on Monday afternoon when reporters suddenly came up to Rev. Smith asking him if we had heard that a verdict had been delivered. They said Johnnie Cochran, Jr., and Marcia Clark weren't even in the building, and they wanted to know Rev. Smith's response to the news. (His clerical collar had become a familiar sight to the reporters, who all knew us.)

On Tuesday, we were again praying alone in the cafeteria when everything broke loose. Despite the wild celebrations taking place in the streets near the courthouse, the main floor of the courthouse was still deserted and considered off limits to the general public. Just as we began to leave the cafeteria to make our way out of the building, the main elevator doors suddenly opened.

The entire defense team was on the elevator, along with the two sheriff's deputies who had been such good friends to us over the last year. The deputies had shocked looks on their faces and they later told us there was absolutely no logical explanation for why that elevator stopped at the main floor that afternoon. When it did stop, seemingly of its own accord, the deputies pushed every button they could push to get it moving again. They were under orders to escort the attorneys quickly and safely to their vehicles so they could exit the building with the least chance of encountering hostile reactions or over-jubilant fans outside.

When johnnie Cochran, Jr., saw us, he stepped out of the elevator with his wife, Dale, and walked over to us. He warmly greeted us and said, "Thank you." We prayed with the entire team of attorneys once again, and made a special effort to thank defense attorney Carl Douglas for his cooperation in our assignment. Douglas is a Christian with a strong witness for Christ. He too had been praying for the various members of the defense team, as well as for the prosecutors and family members on both sides of the case.

We were relieved that a verdict had been delivered, but I knew my work wasn't complete. The OJ. Simpson murder trial had left a lot of casualties in its wake. The trial had taken such a toll on the jury members that Los Angeles County provided psychological counseling for the 12 jury members and two alternates after the trial. The courtroom battles were so acrid that 500 apologies were entered on the court record or given in public to the news media. (That doesn't include all of the insults and threats made during the court proceedings.) Alan Dershowitz was one of the nationally recognized defense attorneys on the "Dream Team." Although he was less visible due to his behind-the-scenes role, Dershowitz nevertheless managed to twice enrage the Fraternal Order of Police with his claims on two different national TV programs that police are "taught to lie."

Christopher Darden was so disillusioned that he told a reporter for *The Los Angeles Times* that he was "ashamed" to be a part of the Simpson case (although he said he wasn't ashamed of the prosecution team). At the time, his faith in the system was so shaken that he doubted if he would even continue to practice law. Later on, he told African-American media professionals at a convention of the National Association of Black Journalists that his concern for victims of violent crimes was the only thing that kept him on the job as a deputy district attorney. Many of the attorneys and jury members in the trial have written books about their experiences in the OJ. Simpson murder trial, and the sales of the books by the most prominent authors were duly noted, compared, and ranked each month for the benefit of millions of people who are still fascinated with the O. J Simpson case.

EPILOGUE

Unfortunately, most people and institutions are slow to learn. Despite the national headlines and disapproval the Los Angeles Police Department earned through the Rodney King beating spectacle and the sloppy handling of the OJ. Simpson prosecution, uniformed LAPD officers were still caught red-handed in another scandal after the trial. TV screens around the world flashed living color images of LAPD officers brutally beating unarmed male and female Mexican workers with nightsticks alongside a busy L.A. freeway in broad daylight.

I have continuing concerns about O. J. Simpson, the victim's family members, and many of the attorneys I met or prayed for during those long months of the trial. Again, God's will for the trial of OJ. Simpson goes far beyond any verdict or assessment of his true guilt or innocence. God knows all of us will come face-to—face with the truth, and with the consequences of the truth in His time. He is concerned with justice nationwide. '

The O. J. Simpson case put the entire nation on trial. It indicted religious institutions and individuals who have "looked the other way" for centuries. It brought the heat of public scrutiny upon the "good ole boy" networks that secretly drive our most revered public institutions with a faulty sense of direction and bankrupt moral values. It uncovered ignored stress cracks and serious foundational flaws in the U.S. legal system. When God shed His light on America's unclean condition (it could have just as easily been my nation of Canada, or any other nation in the world), the nation could no longer continue with "business as usual." His examination has revealed just how sick we are. Now comes a season of reflection, correction, and healing.

Reformation comes slowly, but once the truth is out, if courageous people continue to demand repentance and change, then reformation will come. At the time of this writing, O. J. Simpson is facing more court battles. The family of Ronald Goldman filed a "wrongful death " lawsuit against Simpson in civil court seeking an undetermined amount in damages. (Simpson cannot be retried on criminal charges.) Simpson will also be in court battling with the surviving family members of Nicole Brown Simpson for permanent custody of his children.

I told Rev. Smith many times that I just couldn't accept another "prayer assignment" like the one I just went through, but I knew better. I can't escape the strong sense that God is once again calling me to pray for both of these court cases. I have no idea how; I don't have the financial resources or the physical strength to do it. But then again, can I ignore the call of God? It is obvious that He is not finished with O. J. Simpson, nor is He finished with the Goldman and Brown family members.

I have now accepted the inevitable—somehow, someway, I will be in Los Angeles for the new round of "OJ. trials." I also know that redemptive and healing miracles lie ahead for the grieving members of all three wounded families caught up in this web of pain. For divine reasons and future events I don't fully understand yet, God wants me to continue to pray for them all.

Again, He has instructed me to remain totally neutral for this new assignment. Whatever the future may hold, of this much I am absolutely certain: God is moving to restore righteousness and wholeness to the United States of America. He will continue to shake and cleanse her major institutions just as He has shaken His Church. May we all be willing to obediently fulfill our part in His plan for this land.

If the events and insights in this book have stirred you and created hunger in your heart, then I urge you to do something about it. I wrote this book to reveal God in the affairs of this nation, of the courts, and in the lives of people like you and me. He cares for you and He has a wonderful plan for your life—your birth was no "accident"! Yet God reserves the right, as the Creator, to require each of us to come on His terms.

No one comes to Him in "perfect" condition. Come to Him right now just as you are, and He will help you become what you were destined to be. Whether you are the President of the United States, a fashion designer, a famous sports figure, or a convicted murderer facing the death penalty, if you pray this prayer from your heart right now, God will meet you and save your soul no matter where you are.

A Prayer From the Heart

Dear God,

I come to You in the name of Your Son, Jesus Christ. Your Son said, "The one who comes to Me I will by no means cast out, " so I know You want me to come to You. Thank You for the heavenly invitation that says, "whoever calls on that name of the Lord shall be saved. " I am calling on Your holy name now.

I know I have sinned and I admit it to You. I need Your help to change. The Bible says, "If you confess with your mouth the Lord Jesus and believe in your heart that God has raised Hi from the dead, you will be saved. For with the heart one believes unto righteousness, and with the mouth confession made unto salvation. "

I confess right now that Jesus Christ is my Lord, and that He has made me righteous. Thank You for saving me, Lord Jesus!

Signed ______________________________

Date ______________________________

(Based on John 6:37; Romans 10:13; 10:9—10; 2 Corinthians 5:21, NKJV.)

Now is it important that you tell someone you trust about your prayer for salvation, and for you to find a church home where the church leaders really preach about and live for Jesus Christ, the Son of God. Your life just took a turn for the very best! Welcome home and welcome to God's family!

www.ingramcontent.com/pod-product-compliance
Lightning Source LLC
Chambersburg PA
CBHW070803100426
42742CB00012B/2235

* 9 7 8 1 5 6 0 4 3 2 8 0 7 *